IN THE HOUSE OF FRIENDS

In the House of Friends

Understanding and Healing
from Spiritual Abuse in Christian Churches

KENNETH J. GARRETT

Foreword by
Michael D. Langone

WIPF & STOCK · Eugene, Oregon

IN THE HOUSE OF FRIENDS
Understanding and Healing from Spiritual Abuse in Christian Churches

Wipf & Stock
An Imprint of Wipf and Stock Publishers
199 W. 8th Ave., Suite 3
Eugene, OR 97401

www.wipfandstock.com

PAPERBACK ISBN: 978-1-7252-6602-5
HARDCOVER ISBN: 978-1-7252-6603-2
EBOOK ISBN: 978-1-7252-6604-9

Manufactured in the U.S.A.   JULY 7, 2020

DEDICATION

To the many who are torn down, worn down, and weakened
by abusive pastors and the churches they control.

To the Seven: Amy, Emily, Jessica, Jennifer, Bryn, Rachel, and
Shannon; bright Morning Stars of the MeToo reformation.

To the one who has fled a toxic church for the safety of the
wilds; doubting, wishing, and wondering if his absence has
been noticed by the One who is called a Good Shepherd.

To my dear Lord Jesus, who found me—broken, tattered and
torn, picked me up, held me, and whispered my name in love.

Table of Contents

Foreword

IN THE EARLY 1980S, when I was new to the cultic studies field, my colleagues at International Cultic Studies Association (ICSA— then known as American Family Foundation) and I were approached by national leaders of InterVarsity Christian Fellowship (IV). They were concerned that some of their campus evangelists were becoming too eager, cult-like even. They came to us, a secular psychological organization, because they realized the behaviors that troubled them were not the result of incorrect doctrine. One IV leader, analogizing to the trope of the gunslinger who puts a notch on his gun for every man he kills, said that some of their young people seemed to be putting a notch on their Bible for every soul they supposedly saved. The IV leaders knew that something was wrong. They knew the problem wasn't doctrine. They knew that some people approached by their IV evangelists accused them of being cultists. They hoped that cult specialists might help them better understand what was going on and how to fix it.[1]

In our discussions with IV, it became clear that there were three common ways of defining *cult*. The public and media tended to view *cult* as connoting extreme deviance or weirdness. Religiously inclined persons tended to define a cult as a group that strays too far from orthodox doctrine, in essence a heresy. Mental health professionals who had worked with victims of groups accused of being cults put the emphasis on the use of manipulative,

---

1. Langone, "Cults, Evangelicals, and the Ethics of Social Influence."

controlling, and coercive techniques of influence to induce a pseu-do-conversion characterized by subservience to a leader.

The mental health view sees cultic behavior, what we may also call cultic dynamics, as an area on a continuum of influence going from respectful to manipulative to controlling. Depending upon the circumstances, one may reach an area on this continuum where the influence becomes unethical, where decent people of whatever faith say, "That is wrong. People should not be treated like that."

Some people slide into unethical influence because of undis-ciplined enthusiasm. Their desire to reach an end is so strong that they employ means that, ironically, may be incompatible with the end they seek. This was the case with the IV campus evangelists. Their intentions were good, but the results of their actions were dubious or even harmful. These young evangelists lost sight of a central tenet of Christianity: God gave human beings the freedom to choose good or evil. Therefore, respecting the freedom of indi-viduals—the freedom to say "no" to an evangelizing message, as well as "yes"—is vital in all Christian interactions. Evangelists are witnesses to the gospel. They are not salesmen for Christ.

Other people may use unethical influence tactics because of a corrupt or sinful motive. A pastor, for example, may so de-sire that his church be "successful" (i.e., attract large numbers of people) that he employs promotional tactics that make used-car salesmen blush. This pastor may teach orthodox theology. He may be a sincere and devout Christian. He may say that he is a sinner like everybody else. But he is blind to the compulsive pride that causes his behavior to stray far from the path that Christians are supposed to walk.

Still other people may use unethical influence tactics with full awareness of what they are doing and why. These are the psy-chopaths and malignant narcissists who take advantage of trusting people seeking to improve the world or themselves. These wicked persons may be adept at playing the role of the holy man or woman. While in that role, they may temporarily convince themselves that they are that person. But when they have quiet time alone, they remember who they really are. Unlike Christians who awake to their sinful self-delusion, these con men and women feel no guilt. They believe they are entitled to the spoils their lies bring them because they are so much smarter than the people whom they view as witless fools inviting exploitation.

In my forty years working with victims of cultic groups, I have encountered thousands of people—most of above average intelligence—who have been harmed in the range of manipulative situations from which the three preceding examples are drawn. Approximately 70 percent of those entering the ICSA network were harmed in religious groups. The other 30 percent were harmed in cultic psychotherapies, political groups, new-age transformational trainings, commercial organizations, or families or dyads characterized by a cultic dynamic.

Using the term *cult* has sometimes impeded our work because the term means different things to different people. This has been especially true in the case of people leaving aberrant Christian groups or dysfunctional Christian relationships. Because these victims often conceptualize *cult* as heresy and because they have often been involved in what is ostensibly orthodox Christianity, they tend to ignore organizations that talk about cults.

These persons, however, will often respond to the concept of spiritual abuse. If one has been treated like an object to be manipulated, exploited, and discarded, even if one is only partly aware of the mistreatment, one inevitably feels abused. And if one feels this abuse deep in one's being, in one's soul, or if the abuse occurred in a religious setting, placing the adjective *spiritual* in front of abuse seems apt.

Because so many people entering the ICSA network come from aberrant Christian groups or relationships, we have developed resources that focus on spiritual abuse, most notably www. spiritualabuseresources.com. One section of this website deals with research, of which there is precious little.

A study by the late Rev. Dr. Richard Dowhower[2] surveyed 265 people, most of whom were former members of cultic groups.

2. Dowhower, "Results of the International Cultic Studies Association's 2008 Questionnaire."

The most telling finding of this survey was that "eighty respondents (42%) sought help from mainline religious organizations. Thirty-two persons (40%) found these services not at all helpful." Almost half of the former cult members entering our network sought help from churches, but 40 percent of these help-seekers gave the churches the absolute lowest rating, "not at all helpful." Churches need to be educated about spiritual abuse and cultic dynamics.

Another study that I conducted with the help of Rev. Robert Pardon, director of the New England Institute of Religious Research, surveyed four evangelical churches in southeastern Massachusetts. The total population of the four churches was about 565. Approximately 10 percent of the congregants completed a survey that inquired into their experience of spiritual abuse. Here are the key findings pertinent to this discussion:

The most important question for this report is the number of people who believe they had been "affiliated with a group, organization, or individual that you believe was spiritually abusive." Thirteen of the fifty-five respondents (24 percent) said "yes"; four of the thirteen said the abuse had occurred "in a mainstream church denomination."[3]

Even if none of the 90 percent of church members who did *not* complete the survey had experienced spiritual abuse (which is very unlikely), 2.5 percent of the church members had been spiritually abused. If extrapolated to the US population, this finding suggests that millions of American Christians have been spiritually abused.

What can we conclude?

(a) Advocating orthodox Christian theology does not immunize us against sin.

(b) However well-intentioned one may be, undisciplined enthusiasm for one's faith can cause one to behave in ways that constitute spiritual abuse of those we may claim to love.

---

3. Langone, "Research Survey on Spiritual Abuse."

(c) We are all at risk of succumbing to pride and its constant companion, self-deception. Pride may tempt us to spiritually abuse others by treating them as manipulable objects that serve our pride and obscure our self-deception.

(d) Some people in the world are evil; they hurt and exploit others with awareness and intentionality. Churches must teach their congregations, and especially their youth, how to recognize these spiritual abusers and the deceptively appealing fantasies they promote.

(e) Churches must improve their understanding of spiritual abuse and must learn how to help the "wounded sheep" who may come into their church. The finding that 40 percent of former cult members received "no help at all" from churches should be a call to action for all churches.

(f) Victims of spiritual abuse need help now.

I hope this brief foreword demonstrates why Ken Garrett's book is important. My goal has not been to describe spiritual abuse or explain how to help victims. Ken addresses those issues in detail. His book is a valuable resource for victims and for pastors, seminarians, youth ministers, church members, and families or friends concerned about a loved one caught up in an abusive situation. He effectively weaves together a compelling personal story, testimonies of other spiritual abuse victims, and clear explanations of what spiritual abuse is, how people get sucked into abusive churches, why they stay in abusive relationships, what kind of help they need when they leave, and how churches can become safe havens for the spiritually abused.

If you are a spiritual abuse victim, or a concerned family member or friend of a victim, you will find much solace and wisdom in the pages that follow.

If you are a pastor, seminarian, youth minister, or church member, you have begun to answer the call to action implicit in Rev. Dr. Dowhower's research. Churches must do better than providing "no help at all" to nearly half of the spiritually abused persons who come to them for help.

Michael D. Langone, PhD
Executive Director
International Cultic Studies Association

Prologue: Why I Am Here

2015

THE ROOM IS TOO warm for the end of April. No air condition-ing, and the fan in the corner whirs on its highest setting, but fails to stir the thick, stale air. My long-sleeved shirt feels like a wool sweater.

Most everyone in the room appears uncomfortable, awk-ward, anxious, tense:

. . . the reporter, the photographer, and the court clerk.

. . . the deputies, standing against a wall, their faces dull and passionless. They've seen this show, plenty of times—the words and reactions that will unfold in this room are simply new actors reading an old script.

. . . the deputy district attorney—who, along with the defense attorney, seem to be the only relaxed people in the room. Neither are rookies in this game.

. . . the twelve jurors, sitting still as if they are waiting for a funeral to begin. They steeled themselves for discomfort and unpleasantness.

And above us all is the judge—busy, stern, and serious, her hair as black as her robe.

My family (minus Gracie, who is studying in Russia) is here:

. . . Sharon, thirty-four years married to me.

. . . Brynny and Rachey, both so beautiful, and today so seri-ous. Sometimes they look like twins; but I'm their father, and to me they are perfectly, beautifully distinct from each other. As I look at them at this moment, I see thirty years at once—holding them as infants; worrying about them; sending them off to school, camps, softball, swimming; My Little Pony and Birthday Bear phases, Happy Meals, pizza, boyfriends, cars, jobs, Christmases, Thanksgivings. All the events, big and small, that tell the story of raising kids. My daughters, both of them witnesses, both of them victims. And there are the rest, witnesses and victims—Amy, Emily, Jessica, Jennifer, and Shannon. They are all as close as sisters and are all like daughters to me. They sit, tall and straight, with a seriousness that makes me both proud and sad.

My friends are also here around me: Carole, Dave, Becki, Jean, Paul, Roger, Melody, and many others. All on this side of the room, trying to find comfort on the hard, well-worn, wooden chairs that promise stiff backs and achy hips for all. We're all growing older together.

On the other side of the courtroom from where we sit are old friends whom I haven't seen for many years: Randy and Tami, Bill and Karen, Russ, Gordy, Andy, and a dozen more. They all look tired, tense, and stiff. Dressed for success, the men wear dark suits and ties, as if they're lawyers, bankers, or brokers. The women wear fine dresses, as if they're attending a wedding or some other formal occasion. We were all good friends, too, years ago. But they would not call me a friend today.

Another man also sits apart, in front, his back to us all. He wears a dark business suit, white starched shirt, cuff links, silk tie, and glossy-shined shoes. He carries a small book in his hand. He leans aside and whispers in his lawyer's ear. He turns to his friends seated behind him—my old friends. He smiles and gives a quick, cocky nod of assurance. As he turns, he seems blind to everyone on my side of the room. I look at him closely. I realize that under it all—the clothes, shoes, and attitude—he is small, thin, grey, and sickly looking; and his suit hangs more as drapery than apparel.

He is a man facing trial. He and his friends have paid a fortune to a well-known, often successful defense lawyer. He has said emphatically that he is not a bully or an addict or a drunk or a womanizer.

He has helped poor people and counseled professionals. He is a combat veteran. He has been a leader in his community for more than thirty years. He is well-read. He is intelligent. He is a leader. He is poised. He is a pastor, for goodness sake! He is sure he'll prevail and return to his friends, his wife, his job, his life.

He is why I'm here.

Chapter 1

Cults and Churches . . .

MY PARTNER AND I were driving in our ambulance down a street in Portland, having just completed a call. We picked up on our pre-call conversation, which was me sharing with her about my experience of membership in a small, fundamentalist, high-control, nasty little church—my nasty little *Bible church*. I told her of betrayed friendship, marriages, unprotected children, estranged relatives and non-church fiends, constant pressure to give more time, more money, more loyalty, more, more, more, of everything—over to the church.

"Well, thank the Lord you weren't in a cult, anyway. *That* would have only made things worse."

"How so?" I asked. "I mean, how would things have been worse?"

"Well," she continued, "on top of all the behaviors, sins, trouble with law, alienation from family and pressure—it would have been even worse if you'd been involved in a group with a weird, cultish theology, like the Moonies, or the Mormons, or Krishnas, or those poor people down in Waco, or in Jonest—"

"Yeah, I get it," I said. "At least *we* were Christian, right."

"Right! At least you were Christian, so you know you have the power of God to help you heal and help your family recover. And, at least your church taught the Bible and believed in Jesus. When it all comes down to it, *that's* what counts. Does a church believe in the Bible, and Jesus, or do they not. That's the whole ball of wax, right there. If a church has those two things, it cannot be a cult. It might be a lot *like* a cult, even cult*ish*, but not a cult."

"By this you know the Spirit of God, that every spirit that confesses that Jesus Christ has come—"

"—in the flesh" my friend interrupted. "In the flesh, Ken."

She continued, "You see, Ken, everyone who does not confess Jesus is simply not from God. Not . . . from . . . God. As horrible as your church sounds like it got—did it ever deny the divinity or the humanity of Jesus Christ?"

"No," I answered. "Never. I've always been clear on that, and never really wondered if I, or that church, was Christian. I just never thought of it as being like a cult, and I'm starting to question why it's so important to us that we describe horrible churches as being *like* a cult, cult-like—and seem so intent on preserving some shred of legitimacy, some dignity, when we describe churches that are obviously cultic. It's almost like we think Christianity itself would somehow fall from some lofty state if it had to admit that it had been infiltrated by leaders who built churches, and took over churches, and made them more cults than churches."

"Whoa, whoa, whoa, Kenny. You're opening the door to the idea that a cult is a place where people are treated badly, but you're not referring to its *beliefs*, at least not overtly. Do you think a group can deny Christian doctrine, even Jesus himself, and the Bible, and call itself a church?!"

"I don't know. I'm spending more time these days wondering how a church that acts like a cult can somehow argue that it's not a cult. Maybe it's both. Christian and cult. A Christian cult."

"Ken, I don't think that's possible."

"I know. But it happened. It happened to me."

The final project for my doctor of ministry degree, "Spiritual Abuse in the Church: A Guide to Recognition and Recovery," has three chapters devoted to the question of whether or not an unhealthy, hurtful church that abuses its members should simply be called a *cult*. I wrote of the history of cultic studies and drew the distinctions between a Christian church or group that hurts its

members and a non-Christian group that abuses its members—
and is generally thought of as a cult.

But as my studies progressed, I observed that from a func-
tional standpoint, there is no great difference at all between the
Christian church that ostensibly holds to sound, orthodox beliefs
and the most far-out, bizarre (to me, anyway) cult. One might
be more tied down with moralistic, straight-jacketed rules and
traditions than the other—but both exercise a soul-crushing
subjugation of members. Both are usually led by the same sort
of narcissistic, autocratic leaders who are clever, persuasive, and
charismatic. Both, without exception, are emotionally diseased.
Both promise heaven but deliver hell. Both direct the attention
of members to the eternal promises of abundant blessings, peace,
and power, while their day-to-day experience becomes one of
breathless busyness, emotional fatigue, fracturing marriages and
families, depleting bank accounts, and spiritual starvation. Both
are horrible places for families and children.

I recall my Christian friends and family visiting the small
church that Sharon and I had joined. They evaluated our doctrine
as being sound, and pretty much what they understood to be orthodox. They commented that our commitment to live as followers
of Jesus was admirable, even a clear indication of our conviction.
We were living out what we believed: active in Bible study, church
activities and classes, and in speaking of our faith to those who did
not share it.

However, though our family and friends were experienced,
mature Christians, none of them considered joining our church.
None of them ever recommended the church to their friends
or other family members. They eventually shared with us their
unease with the church's excessive demands on the time and resources of our young marriage and growing family. They timidly
mentioned the changes they'd noted in us—changes for which they
suspected the church was responsible. And they were right: We
were quickly becoming intolerant, moralistic prigs, eagerly exer-
cising what seemed a spiritual gift of ruining every family gathering we attended. As years passed, they also noted the inevitable

religious burnout that we suffered as we turned into self-indulgent, depressed, and dissipated wrecks. But they struggled in using the word *cult* to describe us. The furthest they would go was to say, "You almost seem to act like you're in a cult, Kenny." That "C" word is powerful but poorly defined, and, in the minds of many, never to be suggested of a Christian church.

I believe this reticence to consider that a Christian church could actually be a cult (with good doctrine, nonetheless!) continues. Often, our limited understanding of the qualities of a cult have not served us well to recognize those dynamics in unexpected contexts. I use the term *abusive church* in this book to describe the hurtful, malignant churches that I describe. I do this because I'm not really interested in pushing anyone into a corner to admit, "OK, Ken; I was in a cult." But make no mistake: When I write of abusive churches, I am at the very least describing churches that treat their members in a destructive, *cultic* manner. They are cults disguised as churches, or churches that have become cults.

Chapter 2

Spiritual Abuse . . . *in the Bible?*

DO YOU THINK THE Bible is full of sanctified saints who lived spotless lives, walked 18 inches off the ground before they died and went to heaven, where they inherited golden harps and reserved seats on a heavenly clouds? Think again. *TMZ*, the *National Enquirer*, the *internet*, and any other gossip source haven't got a thing on the sins, foibles, and missteps of the people of God as described in the Bible. Its pages are replete with accounts of betrayal, swindling, lying, violence, political intrigue, marriage troubles, and moral compromise, and they leave little to the imagination. Alongside these brutal and often salacious sins are numerous accounts of the misuse of power in which bullying, unscrupulous leaders take advantage of well-intentioned, religious-minded folks. Let's consider a few examples.

Hophni and Phineas were two sons of Eli, the high priest of Israel. They served in the tabernacle-shrine of the nation, located in a small village called Shiloh. Taking advantage of their family's position in the religious life of Israel, the sons routinely stole the sacrifices brought by their fellow Israelites who came to worship at Shiloh. Instead of offering the choice meat brought to the tabernacle to be offered up in worship, Hophni and Phineas took the meat home for themselves. Instead of receiving valuable gifts of support for the tabernacle ministry—they stole them. And they also slept with the women who volunteered to assist in the tabernacle worship rituals and services. They used their religious authority for material gain and sexual gratification. In doing so, they became abusers of the very people they were supposed to serve and protect. Today, spiritual leaders who use their pedigree, power, and position in the church to satisfy their personal desires at the expense of the members of the church are following in the footsteps of Hophni and Phineas.

David was a middle-aged, slightly out-of-shape king who had stopped leading his armies in battle, and instead remained behind in the relative safety and comfort of the palace in Jerusalem. One night, David was unable to sleep and rose from his bed to walk around his palace, which overlooked the city. It also overlooked the home of one of his top generals, Uriah. David saw Uriah's wife, Bathsheba, bathing. Stimulated at the sight of her naked body, David did something horrible—seemingly without thought, as if he had done it many times before. He sent a servant to fetch Bathsheba to the palace so he could sleep with her. She arrived, they had sex, and David sent her home. But she had conceived a child with the king. In an attempt to conceal the parentage of the baby, David ordered Bathsheba's husband, Uriah, home from the war. David presumed that Uriah would doubtlessly sleep with his wife Bathsheba—thus creating a perfectly plausible explanation for her pregnancy. But Uriah refused to enjoy the comforts of home and spouse, and instead slept outside the palace, with the king's servants. He was unwilling to kick up his heels and relax while the men he commanded were at war, living in peril, sleeping in the open. It's almost as if Uriah was saying, "Get the point, David? This is how a leader lives and acts."

Instead, David got the point that his cover-up had failed, and Uriah would certainly know that he was not the father of Bathsheba's child. So David schemed to send Uriah back to the front and to be sent on a suicide mission that ensured his death in combat. Uriah died alone in a firestorm of Aramean arrows. David's plan seemed to work—for a little while. Today, when Christian leaders take advantage of the loyalty and commitment of their church members, sexually abuse them and attack their marriages, they are following in the footsteps of the out-of-shape, middle-aged King David. Like the ancient king, they are taking what is not theirs to have, simply because they want to and they can.

The corrupt spiritual leaders of ancient Israel are likened to voracious, greedy, violent shepherds who used their flocks for personal enrichment:

> Then the word of the LORD came to me saying, "Son of man, prophesy against the shepherds of Israel. Prophesy and say to those shepherds, 'Thus says the Lord GOD, "Woe, shepherds of Israel who have been feeding themselves! Should not the shepherds feed the flock? You eat the fat and clothe yourselves with the wool, you slaughter the fat sheep without feeding the flock.""[1]

It was common in ancient Near Eastern cultures to identify rulers, kings, and leaders as shepherds over the people they led. But these religious leaders were like dishonest, thieving shepherds, who drank the milk of the flock, stole its wool, and butchered its choicest animals to provide rich meals for themselves as the flock itself starved and withered. These abusive *spiritual* shepherds had stolen the resources of God's flock—their fellow Jews.

> Therefore, you shepherds, hear the word of the LORD: "As I live," declares the Lord GOD, "surely because My flock has become a prey, My flock has even become food for all the beasts of the field for lack of a shepherd, and My shepherds did not search for My flock, but rather the shepherds fed themselves and did not feed My flock."[2]

Just as the lazy, self-indulgent shepherds were unwilling to face the dangers and difficulties of the wilderness to search for and rescue those sheep that were scattered and isolated from the flock, the corrupt, self-centered leaders of Israel had no compassion or concern for the isolated, alienating experience of those Jews who'd become marginalized from their religion and community.

---

1. Ezek 34:1–3. Unless otherwise noted, biblical quotations are from the New American Standard Version (Updated).

2. Ezek 34:7–8.

Therefore, thus says the Lord GOD to them, "Behold, I, even I, will judge between the fat sheep and the lean sheep. Because you push with side and with shoulder, and thrust at all the weak with your horns until you have scattered them abroad, therefore, I will deliver My flock, and they will no longer be a prey; and I will judge between one sheep and another."[3]

In Ezekiel's prophetic accusation, the worthless shepherds allowed healthy, robust animals to bully and mistreat the weaker ones, just as Israel's abusive spiritual leaders looked the other way when bullies in the community took advantage of their poor, weak, and marginalized fellow citizens. Today, the self-serving, often aggressive speech of abusive religious leaders has the same effect, with these leaders panting over the resources and wealth of wealthier members, empowering their fellow abusers, and attacking the brave few who dare to challenge their behavior.

As the Bible unfolds, from the life of Jesus of Nazareth to the birth and expansion of the early Christian church, abusive spiritual leaders are always on the scene, attacking the very faith communities they were supposed to serve.

Jesus startled his listeners in the first few minutes of the longest recorded sermon he preached by assuring them that their moral conduct must exceed that of their religious leaders if they had any hope of gaining heaven. "Unless your righteousness surpasses that of the scribes and Pharisees, you will not enter the kingdom of heaven."[4] He concluded the sermon with the sobering warning to "beware of the false prophets, who come to you in

3. Ezek 34:20–22.

4. Matt 5:20 and following. The scribes and Pharisees were two prominent religious groups in ancient Israel. They worked closely with each other in shaping the religious life of the people. Scribes were religious scholars that specialized in the study and application of the various traditions developed by Jewish scholars and rabbis over the centuries. Pharisees were religious conservatives who demanded strict, hyperliteral adherence to both Jewish scriptures and the traditions that arose from them. They held great power over the common people of Israel, and had significant influence with the Roman governors who ruled the nation.

sheep's clothing, but inwardly are ravenous wolves."[5] Scribes and Pharisees were the most religious people his listeners knew! Who had it all together more than those guys?

Matthew 24 records the barrage of charges that Jesus laid down against the spiritual abusers of Israel. They concocted burdensome religious demands for their followers but would not lift a finger to help them bear those burdens (v. 4). They loved being noticed as religious leaders, honored in public, and granted powerful titles (vv. 5–12). They spoke as authoritative gatekeepers of the kingdom of heaven, though they themselves would not enter it (v. 13). They took financial advantage of the poor and marginalized of their day, all the while reveling in pretentious, long, very public prayers (v. 14). They went to over-the-top extremes to recruit followers, whom they then trained to be as profane and hypercritical as themselves (v. 15). They used spiritual truths and religiosity to gain material resources for themselves (vv. 16–22). They gave meticulous attention to the observance of the most minute, intricate aspects of their religion, but they ignored its deeper, "weightier" provisions, such as the practices of "justice and mercy and faithfulness" (vv. 23–24). They maintained an obvious, external appearance of morality and righteousness, but inwardly they were filthy and corrupt, full of hypocrisy and lawlessness (vv. 25–28). They made a great show of honoring and decorating the memorials and gravesites of the nation's historic prophets, as if they would have been ardent supporters had they lived in their days, but it was actually their own order of ecclesial religious leaders who had murdered those very prophets (vv. 29–39)! It is no wonder that, as Jesus's public ministry progressed, their disdain for him increased, leading them to expel his followers from their synagogues and to devise plots against him that ultimately led to his arrest and death.[6] They simply hated him. Today, when you see a pastor or church leader cite his position, education, or reputation as justification to bring hardship, pain, and loss into the lives of those who simply

---

5. Matt 7:15.

6. John 9:22; 12:42; Matt 7:13–20; 9:11, 34; 23:1–39; Mark 7:5-13; Luke 6:7–11; John 11:46-53.

seek to follow Jesus, you are witnessing the ongoing *ministry crimes* of the scribes and Pharisees.

As the New Testament unfolds, its writers give repeated warning concerning the threat of abusive leaders in the ancient Near Eastern, Mediterranean world. From its earliest days, unscrupulous, spiritually abusive leaders threatened the Christian church. Speaking to a group of pastors, the Apostle Paul warned,

> Be on guard for yourselves and for all the flock, among which the Holy Spirit has made you overseers, to shepherd the church of God which He purchased with His own blood. I know that after my departure savage wolves will come in among you, not sparing the flock; and from among your own selves men will arise, speaking perverse things, to draw away the disciples after them.[7]

Like shepherds constantly watching out for wolves and wild dogs, these pastors were to remain on the alert, always guarding their congregations against attacks from spiritual predators. And Paul's words were not spoken as mere contingency. The apostle was certain that, after he had departed, their churches would face an onslaught of abusive, predatory leaders seeking to gain followers, and the resources of those followers. His warning was stark and pressing. The attackers were coming, and their behavior would be stealthy, cunning, and savage.

Paul's letters to churches and to his fellow leaders are rich with accounts of the unfolding of his ominous prophecy, a prophecy that continues to this day as unscrupulous, power-hungry leaders dominate and abuse church members. He warned the churches he started across the ancient Mediterranean world of the ever-present threat of abusive leaders. He confronted members of the church of Corinth regarding false leaders who had taken positions of authority in the church, marveling at the willingness of the Corinthians to submit themselves to severe spiritual abuse.[8] He unleashed some of his most forceful invective against Jewish teachers who had entered the churches of Galatia and sought to

7. Acts 20:28–30.

8. 2 Cor 11:13, 20.

impose the traditions and religious laws of Judaism on the Gentile Christians in that region.[9] The letters Paul wrote to Timothy and Titus (pastors whom he had trained) are largely concerned about abusive leaders who had gained positions of power and influence and were troubling the members in the churches that Timothy and Titus led. Paul reminded Timothy that the rise of abusive leaders—"liars seared in their own conscience as with a branding iron"—was a matter of prophetic certainty, and that these men would impose ascetic demands on their followers.[10]

Paul's letter to his fellow pastor Titus bears the same concern for the damage done to church members by abusive leaders. Paul explained the importance and immediacy of Titus's task, and again, identified characteristics common to abusive leaders: rebelliousness, lack of substance in speech, deceitfulness, and the tendency of upsetting families through errant, greed-driven instruction:

> For there are many rebellious men, empty talkers and deceivers, especially those of the circumcision, who must be silenced because they are upsetting whole families, teaching things they should not teach for the sake of sordid gain.[11]

These were leaders who liked to fight, loved to hear themselves talk, and misled people regarding how to have healthy relationships—both with God and with other people. They caused discord in families and would say anything to get their hands on the money of their followers. The letters of Peter, John, and Jude

---

9. Gal 1:8–9; 3:1; 4:17; 6:12–13. From its earliest days, as it arose out of Judaism, the Christian church had engaged in discussion and debate with Jewish teachers who sought to understand and test the claims of the Christian faith (i.e., Acts 17:10–11; 18:19; 24–26; 28:17 and following). Sadly, in the context of this legitimate, necessary theological interchange, there arose unscrupulous Jewish teachers who sought to manipulate and control Gentile Christian converts, and to be enriched at their expense. It is against the damage inflicted by these malicious quasi-Jewish teachers that Paul warns his readers.

10. 1 Tim 4:1–3.

11. Titus 1:10–11.

are also largely focused on issues of leadership, and on the damage that abusive leaders pose to a church community.[12]

According to the writers of the New Testament, the greatest threat to the health of churches was not persecution from the government, or the attacks of rival religious groups, or angry mobs who blamed Christians for the troubles of society. It was not a lack of funds or resources. It was not even the absence of effective, state-of-the-art communication systems to broadcast the message of the Christian faith to the world. It was not the church's lack of political or cultural influence. And it was not in the church's lack of great preaching, grand buildings, great crowds, or extensive programs. Although these deficiencies and challenges can be found throughout its two thousand–year history, the greatest threat to any church was, and remains, the presence of abusive pastors and leaders who control members, get rich off the ministry, and corrupt the magnificent, grace-infused message of the Christian faith.

But how do these predators make it into the church, and into positions of power and influence, and access to so much? Obviously, they do not enter into churches with a mask and a gun and demand, "Give me your money, your buildings, your time, your bodies, now!" In fact, the things they take from their church members are usually handed over to them, willingly it seems, by those members. How do these spiritual predators get those things? In the next chapter, we will explore the most powerful tool of the spiritual abuser—a tool that becomes a weapon used against the members of his church: his speech.

12. See esp. 2 Peter; 2 and 3 John; and Jude.

Chapter 3

Abusive Pastors—How They Tick, How They Talk

MOST OF THE SURVIVORS of spiritual abuse who come through the doors of my church have been abused by a pastor. These survivors come from a variety of churches and Christian organizations. They act a bit shy or hesitant, are a bit standoffish, and are in no great hurry to make any commitments to our church—or to any church, for that matter. They watch me very closely, and I get the reason why they do so. There are few times in life where any of us hear a person who is more convinced of what is best for our life than when we hear a preacher preach, or speak with an over-zealous proselytizer for a church or cult. Having belonged to an abusive church, and having endured the long, challenging process of recovery, I understand how disturbing it can be to a survivor of spiritual abuse to sit and listen to a man (it's almost always a man), standing a few feet above the audience, behind a pulpit, holding a Bible, experienced in public speaking, explaining why they should believe what he's saying, and do what he tells them.

I like to think that God himself might send people to my church because they need to find a group of people who will believe their stories of spiritual abuse and will not attribute their accounts as merely the residue of animosity toward their former church and pastor, or even an inability to get along with others.

Without exception, the horrific experiences of the victims that I speak with begin and end with the abusive pastor:

"He told my wife to divorce me—that our marriage was never God's will anyway—and she did. He told my kids not to talk to me or read my letters—and they don't."

"He called the young men who were his interns his 'special, mighty men.' I learned that he was molesting them all."

"He kept asking for more and more money so he would not lose his property—we gave and gave, but we lost our home."

"He told my husband that he was responsible to 'disciple' me—after twenty years of marriage, for goodness' sake!"

"He told my wife it made sense why we were having trouble in our marriage—since I wasn't really as 'serious' about following Jesus as she was."

"He kept demanding more money, but also more time. I did not have time for overtime shifts, and gave away many of my regular shifts, to be at church functions. In the end, I was broke and my credit was shot. I declared bankruptcy."

"He recorded our conversations, and then played them back to the leadership team in a meeting."

"I ran into the pastor at a bookstore, after I left the church. He started hassling me—and actually ordered me to leave the bookstore. Amazing!"

"He sued me when I gave his church a negative review online."

"He told me I could leave the church anytime I wanted to— but my wife would stay, and the entire church would fight to keep the kids with her, not me."

"He told my husband that I was a rebellious woman, and our marriage probably would not last."

"He wanted me to share all kinds of personal information, such as my medical history, relationship history, and sexual history."

"He set things up so that some members were treated differently. They were his favorites members. They were special."

"When he found out my grandparents had left me money in their will, he told me to go visit them every week, and 'stay on their good side.' Later, when they died, he expected me to give the church a large amount of money, like *he* was an heir, and not me!"

"He told everyone how to vote on issues and candidates, and never presented any other political views but his own. He demonized the candidates he didn't like; and the ones he supported, he made them out to be saints, even though it was obvious they weren't even Christians."

"He preached that, if you weren't baptized in his church, you weren't a follower of Jesus."

It is vital that we understand and note both the behavior and the speech of the abusive pastor. Let's face it—we often are fixated on the horrible things we hear of religious phonies doing; and without personal knowledge of such grimy vices, we don't think they could be very abusive, after all. We look instead for secret vices, ostentatious lifestyles, hidden addictions, DUIs, hidden criminal records, paid-off lovers. . . . However, not every spiritual abuser misbehaves or indulges in the more sensual types of sin. Some lead very disciplined, outwardly moral lives while they rule over those who follow them with an iron fist.

So if we don't find any sordid, sinful behaviors that reveal the abusive pastor, what clues might we observe that would suggest he is a spiritual abuser? I believe there are at least three solid indicators of predatory pastors: their mindset, their speech, and their extraction of material, physical, and spiritual resources from those who follow them.

The Mindset of the Abusive Pastor

Spiritual abusers are motivated by unmet desires, often deeply hidden, never acknowledged, and only discovered through the examination of verbal and behavioral evidence. They may be driven by the desire for influence, affirmation, and community power (and all of the control and use of resources entailed in such power). The unbridled love of wealth and material possessions may drive them, or the desire to outperform perceived ideological enemies and supposed competitors. They may seek to demonstrate power though flirting or sexual conquest. They may simply be driven by the desire to escape their own personal sense of inadequacy and unworthiness. They are empty. They need others to fill them.

The ancient Greek poet Ovid wrote of Narcissus, a young man who was a skillful hunter and was known for his physical beauty. He was a proud, unapproachable youth, and he looked down on those who tried to get close to him. One day Narcissus was hunting in the forest. He sensed he was being watched—and he was. A forest fairy named Echo saw the handsome youth and immediately fell in love with him—at a distance. She tentatively followed him into the forest; and when she drew close and spoke with him, he casually rejected her overtures of affection, deeply hurting her feelings. But there was someone else watching Narcissus, too. The goddess Nemesis had viewed the whole affair and was angered at the young man's rejection of Echo. So Nemesis devised a punishment for such cruelty. She drew Narcissus through the trees of the forest to a clear, still pool of water. As he passed by it, Narcissus noticed the inviting pool and was drawn to the remarkably beautiful person he saw in it—himself. Falling in love with his own reflection, he became frustrated every time that he reached out to touch it. The lovely face disappeared in the rings of disturbed water. He was fixated—and he became despondent that his image was unable to return his love. Unwilling to leave his reflection, disappointed and alone, Narcissus died there, gazing at his reflection, and at the same time both desiring and feeling himself desired.[1] The tragic myth of Narcissus is the origin of the term *narcissism*, a fixation with oneself that can be described as a sort of disordered, excessive self-love. A narcissist's tendency is to view others as mere objects to meet their personal craving for recognition, influence, and validation of worthiness. They can become very dark and sinister, and horribly damaging to their victims. The extreme forms of narcissism are part of a recognized personality disorder, narcissistic personality disorder (NPD).[2] When his narcissism takes a malicious turn, the narcissist assaults others (emotionally, and sometimes physically/sexually). NPD has been described by practitioners as *Traumatizing Narcissism*,[3] or *Malignant Narcissism*,[4] or *Malignant Self-Love*.[5]

Unlike the mythical hunter Narcissus, these leaders are not enamored by their own physical appearance (although that is certainly a possibility!). Instead, they are dedicated to the promotion and care of themselves through the subjugation of their followers, and the demand that followers hand over their material and emotional resources. These precious resources, in the hands of the narcissistic pastor, are consumed as he tries to fill his own unfilled, unfillable soul.

1. *Metamorphoses* (A. S. Kline's version), bk. 3, Ovid Collection, University of Virginia, http://ovid.lib.virginia.edu/trans/Metamorph3.htm#476975712.

2. *DSM-5*, 645, 669–72. The Mayo Clinic lists the following symptoms of narcissism: having an exaggerated sense of self-importance; expecting to be recognized as superior even without achievements that warrant it; exaggerating achievements and talents; being preoccupied with fantasies about success, power, brilliance, beauty, or the perfect mate; believing that oneself is superior and able to be understood only by or associated with equally special people; requiring constant admiration; having a sense of entitlement; expecting special favors and unquestioning compliance with expectations; taking advantage of others to get what one wants; having an inability or unwillingness to recognize the needs and feelings of others; being envious of others and believing others envy oneself; behaving in an arrogant or haughty manner.

3. Shaw, *Traumatic Narcissism*.

4. De Canonville, *Three Faces of Evil*.

5. Vaknin, *Malignant Self-Love*.

The Speech of the Abusive Pastor

Most of what pastors do is speak. They say things to people in public and in private, and inevitably their speech reveals what they really believe and who they truly are. The speech of the abusive pastor—not just his sermons, or teaching, or public comments, but *all* his speech—reveals his core identity, or as Jesus put it, "The mouth speaks that which fills the heart" (Matt 12:34). He was aware that actions can appear to be very good, very religious, and yet be performed by leaders whom he considers strangers, and that good things might be done in his name by people who didn't in fact serve him.

> Beware of the false prophets who come to you in sheep's clothing but inwardly are ravenous wolves. You will know them by their fruits. Grapes are not gathered from thorn bushes, nor figs from thistles, are they? So every good tree bears good fruit, but the bad tree bears bad fruit. A good tree cannot produce bad fruit, nor can a bad tree produce good fruit. Every tree that does not bear good fruit is cut down and thrown into the fire. So then you will know them by their fruits.[6]

Jesus taught that false prophets approach a religious community as if they are friendly toward it and are its legitimate leaders. The *sheep's clothing* does not denote the woolen hide of a sheep, but the wool cloak that was worn by shepherds of that day.[7] So, these abusive shepherds would have an external appearance and behavior that argued for their legitimacy. They would look the part. However, their appearance and behavior would actually camouflage their danger and identity, allowing them to easily infiltrate

6. Matt 7:15-20.

7. ἐν ἐνδύμασιν προβάτων: lit., *wear sheep's clothing*; i.e., *only pretending to be harmless*, of the ways of a false teacher, disguising destructive intentions (Friberg et al., *Analytical Lexicon*). "From ancient times to modern days it has often been customary for pastoral people to make for themselves coats out of the skins of the sheep with wool still adhering to the skins" ("Shepherds," Bible History (website), https://www.bible-history.com/links.php?cat=39&sub=414&cat_name=&subcat_name=Shepherds).

the congregations they sought to rule over. He warned that despite their appearance of legitimacy—it was by their *fruits* they would be recognized as predators.

But what exactly *is the fruit of a prophet?*

According to Jesus, it is his speech.

> Not everyone who says to Me, "Lord, Lord," will enter the kingdom of heaven, but he who does the will of My Father who is in heaven will enter. Many will say to Me on that day, "Lord, Lord, did we not prophesy in Your name, and in Your name cast out demons, and in Your name perform many miracles?" And then I will declare to them, "I never knew you; Depart from me, you who practice lawlessness!"[8]

Prophesying, casting out demons, and performing miracles are all things that begin with words of some sort. Without qualification, the true nature of a prophet is known through his speech.[9] *Words* are the fruit of the teacher, and the pastor is a teacher. *Good words* come from good pastors. *Evil words* come from evil pastors.

Every Christian leader, every pastor, eventually reveals his authentic and core values to those around him, as they know him, observe him, and especially as they hear what he says. The distant pastor, perhaps preaching to a large gathering every week, can hide his core identity for years because so few people get close enough to hear him at any other time than when he preaches. But most pastors lead small churches; and over the years, their church members get to know them very well, more through circumstances than sermons. They know the voice of their pastor, for they hear him when he is angry, saddened, hurt, joyful, surprised, disappointed, casual, relaxed, in the pulpit, out of the pulpit, on the street, in front of the church, in his backyard, or conversing over a cup of coffee. His

---

8. Matt 7:21–23.

9. Prophesying, casting out demons, and performing miracles are all primarily acts of speech, of spoken words. If you want a demonstration of what I mean, stand in front of a mirror and act out what you believe to be prophesying, casting out a demon, or performing a miracle. Don't be shy, try it! See what I mean? Regardless of your physical actions—you *said* something, didn't you?

IN THE HOUSE OF FRIENDS

speech and behavior through the years make him known by those he leads. The false prophet of Jesus' day is the abusive, narcissistic pastor today, and over time he betrays his appearance by both his speech and his behaviors, but mostly by the words, all the words, that leave his lips. Sadly, by the time his followers realize the revealing nature of his speech, they often have become trapped in the church he dominates.

Chapter 4

Who Would Ever Join an Abusive Church?

WHO WOULD EVER JOIN a church that functioned like a cult, led by a mentally unhealthy, narcissistic, and abusive pastor? Who would knowingly join a church that demanded its members' time, money, heart, and soul, and yet did not provide any substantive return on such precious investments? What single person, hoping to find a marriage partner, would join a church that controls and determines the selection of a mate, and even presumes to give the couple permission to marry in the first place? Who would join a church that demands parents raise children in strict accordance with the pastor's wishes and beliefs—though he himself may not even have any children of his own? Would anyone join a church that discouraged them from pursuing a better education, career, or the pursuit of legitimate, healthy, lifelong goals and dreams? Who would join a church that demanded its members put the church first, over marriage, family, friendships, and both physical and emotional health?

According to the experts, nobody joins such a church on purpose. They are recruited into them, believing that they have found, or were divinely led to, a church that would serve their desires and goals for the kind of faith—the kind of life—they want as followers of Christ Jesus. They join churches that promise them a better experience of the Christian faith, an experience of the spiritual life that corresponds to the life they feel they need; or that promise them the friendships and social connectedness they crave. Abusive churches never present themselves as spiritual gulags. Instead, they promote themselves as places where members can find community, friendship, spiritual growth, fresh purpose, and assistance with the challenges of life and family.

And those are the very reasons that my wife and I joined a small church that met in a rented house in the spring of 1984. We saw the church as a unique faith community where we would receive help with our young, troubled marriage and the genuine friendships we longed for, in what seemed a distinct, purposeful, spiritually oriented community. Given our particular backgrounds and beliefs about Christianity, the opportunity was an appeal we were almost powerless to ignore.

A friend of mine wrote a wonderful book about her experience in a spiritually abusive church in Texas. In *I Can't Hear God Anymore—Life in a Dallas Cult*, survivor Wendy Duncan does a great job of explaining the powerful appeal of the church she joined, and later found to be abusive:

> Imagine a place where you are accepted and loved, where there is complete honesty and transparency, where you can totally be yourself and no longer have to strive to be someone else. Envision a safe haven where you could live in perfect peace and have everything you needed and wanted. That was the dream—and hope—that Trinity Foundation offered and that we naively believed. We longed for a shelter from the fast-paced lifestyle that surrounded us; we yearned for a harbor of refuge from the stressful concerns of life. We had a vision of living in a community of people who aspired to be like Jesus and to live like the first-century Christians. For those of us who became a part of the group, there was also an intense hunger for spiritual guidance and religious truth, a hunger that was easily exploited. For a brief time in our lives, we believed that we had found true community.[1]

But we need not travel all the way to the Lone Star State to find an example of someone being recruited into an abusive, unhealthy

---

1. Duncan, *I Can't Hear God Anymore*, 35.

church, and willingly throwing themselves into a church that would almost cost them everything they valued in life.

Me, the Totalist

There was something about *me*, not the church, that attracted and compelled me to find the church, whose congregation met in a little red, ranch-style house in a rundown part of town, and whose leadership boasted of its singular commitment to making disciples, so attractive and compelling: I was pathologically attracted to the church's total commitment, the all-or-nothing approach to faith. As a recently discharged paratrooper and medevac medic with the Army, and a newly hired paramedic in a large city, I was highly competitive and motivated to succeed. I pursued everything I did with full abandon, driven by a desire for greatness and significance that was channeled into my Christian faith. I didn't just desire to be a loyal, faithful follower of Jesus—I hungered to be radically committed to him, above and beyond all commitments in life. No price was too high to pay in the pursuit of Christian growth, which (I believed) would make me more likely to one day become a powerful preacher. I was like a light bulb, just waiting for the right sized socket to plug into, so I could burn bright and lead the world to Jesus, through me.

It was 1985, and I was on the campus of a large university where I was attending a missions conference with a group of fellow members of the new church I had just begun to attend. I was twenty-five years old. I had a deep desire to make a mark, to be in vocational ministry. The desire was consuming, gnawing, sincere, and naïve.

I do not recall anything I heard that day about missions. As with most conferences, there were plenary sessions in a large hall where presenters spoke of the current state of affairs in the world of missions ministries, and of the crying need for young people to train as missionaries so they could bring the Christian message to the ends of the earth. There were slick advertising booths set up in another large room where various missions organizations and parachurch ministries provided information on their work, gave out free pens, and distributed notepads and key chains with their organizations' logos on them. For someone who desired a career in Christian ministry, each booth was magical, provocative, and stimulating. I envied those young people who manned the booths of the various ministries, handing out those mission souvenirs. *These* individuals had been called and had found their place. *I* had not. My desire to *do something*, preferably something *very big*, for Jesus, was provoked and encouraged. The larger meetings were punctuated by smaller *breakout* sessions, where speakers introduced their respective organization's mission and talked about what it was doing and hoped to do to take the Christian message to the nations.

My friends and I attended a session that presented a large, multinational Christian organization focused on an area of Christian ministry that we were very excited about—*discipleship*—the training of younger Christians by mature Christians, with the goal of spiritual growth and effectiveness in the Christian ministry. The organization enjoyed a reputation for the seriousness with which it pursued its mission of training faithful, effective followers of Jesus Christ—disciples. Well, this was perfect! *Disciple-making* was just what our little Bible church was all about! We felt that it was pretty much the *only* thing *any* church should be about, really, and that our particular way of making disciples was certainly the exact method used by Jesus himself.

The presenter lived in a good-sized city and was speaking of the organization's ministry at a large university a couple of hours away. He made a compelling argument for the value and challenge of his ministry. He told us of his method of making disciples, which included Bible study and memorization, many one-on-one meetings (in which disciples would report on their successes and failures in following the disciplines and instruction of the Christian faith), evangelistic training, and spiritual mentoring. A significant goal of the ministry was that its members would progress to the point that they themselves would become *disciple makers*, helping (spiritually) younger students progress in their faith. These students would then go on to make disciples themselves. (I know; you're thinking, *Ken, isn't that kind of like the multilevel marketing scheme my brother-in-law lost all of his money in a few years ago?* Well . . . yeah, kind of, and the 6.4 million disciples who I envisioned one day being responsible for never materialized . . .)

Overall, the ministry organization appeared challenging and effective. The presenter was a sharp person. He was intense, articulate, comfortable speaking in front of a crowd, and fully convinced of the importance, effectiveness, and biblical legitimacy of his ministry model, which he described as being a *de facto* continuation of the very ministry model Jesus used in the training of his twelve disciples for ministry. Of all the speakers we heard that weekend, at all the workshops and plenary sessions, I found him the most compelling. I imagined myself one day being that sort of man, speaking with that sort of power and certainty, drawing people who, like me, wanted to be like him!

Beyond these impressions, the specific thing that made the workshop memorable occurred at the end of the session, when the speaker answered various questions about discipleship from the audience.

A young man, about my age, raised his hand and commented, "I live in a small town, and there's no one doing disciple making in my town."

"How do you know that?" asked the disciple maker.

"Uh, I have asked around, and talked to my pastor, and checked at the community college there. It's not going on. What should I do? I mean, if there is no one to disciple me into a person who can make disciples myself, how can I ever actually *do* discipleship?"

The young man was earnest in his desire to find help and training in his spiritual life. The speaker had presented a compelling argument for the absolute necessity of making disciples, just as the Lord and the Apostle Paul did—one at a time, through one-on-one, mentoring relationships. There seemed no other legitimate, biblical way to experience spiritual growth. And so the young man was in search of a disciple maker.

"You are sure about that?" pressed the speaker.

The young man nodded in answer. "Yes, I am."

"Well, then move to my town, and I'll disciple you," he shot back. The room fell silent.

"Uh, that's over a hundred miles from me. That's . . . quite a distance," the would-be (and now, faltering) disciple said.

"Well . . ." The presenter paused. I felt the tension of a challenge laid down, almost as if a dare. I leaned forward in my chair. ". . . I guess it all comes down to how badly you want to be discipled."

There, he said it! He validated the take-no-prisoners, stop-your-whining-and-start-*doing-something* imperative of his ministry. People shifted in their chairs. . . . I imagine some were wondering if they possessed the degree of desire for discipleship that would impel them to move a hundred miles to enter into a mentoring relationship with this man. I imagine some were glad they didn't ask such a question, and that our breakout session was about over. But as for me, it was electrifying to hear it said, right there, right out in the open:

"How bad do you want it . . . *that* bad, really? Prove it, then!"

When I reflect on that breakout session, I believe my response to the awkward interchange reveals why I chose to naively join a church that abused its members. You see, I *liked* the approach of the disciple maker. His answer to the young man's question became a challenge of the man's sincerity—his true desire to be a disciple. Having recently transitioned out of the military, and still struggling to get my civilian legs, I was drawn to the clear, black-and-white, no-nonsense nature of the disciple maker's challenge. It made sense to me. No *ifs*, *ands*, *buts*, or *maybes*. Just:

"How badly do you want to be a disciple?"

Black or white, yes or no; are you in, or are you out? In my heart, I was hard on the young man for his hesitancy and failure to accept the challenge, right there, on the spot. He was reticent to jump at such an opportunity for growth and impact for the kingdom of God. *I would have done it. I would have moved. I would have quit my job, moved my family, and severed all relational ties that held me to a* normal *life of shallow faith. I would have jumped at the opportunity!*

But I did not need to . . . because I already had. I was in the initial months of membership in the church that routinely challenged its members just as the presenter had challenged the young man—total commitment to discipleship, without reservation. All you had to do was attend one of its worship services, and you would catch how serious its pastors and member took their faith.

The church met in a living room, and its twenty-five members sat on folding chairs in three rows. The service followed a traditional, Baptist church format: a welcome and announcements time, a prayer, a couple of hymns, an offering collection, and then the sermon.

I recall the sermon the pastor preached on my first visit to the church. He had titled the sermon "A Furlough of Futility." The sermon was part of a preaching series on the life of King David, and it specifically covered a period when David (before he was king) lived as a mercenary among the enemies of Israel, the Philistines. He hired himself and his soldiers out to the Philistine king to do battle for them, and then lied about his activities.[2] The focus of the sermon was on the frustration, and ultimate failure, of one leaving God's plan for life. To abandon one's commitment to God would inevitably lead to hypocrisy, frustration, and a life of lying and secrets. Packed with historical, cultural insights; observations derived from the Hebrew text itself; and illustrations that seemed to correspond exactly to my own experiences, the sermon was compelling. The pastor preached with fervor, conviction, and

---

2. 1 Sam 27.

charisma. He was young, unpolished, confrontational, and deadly serious about what he was doing.

I sneaked glances at the church members. Each was taking notes, furiously trying to keep up with the preacher. They occasionally interrupted their note-taking to look up and nod (that's about as charismatic as the congregation ever got). No daydreaming, thumbing through hymnals, or making shopping lists here. These people were serious. I felt right at home and would soon be challenged as to just how serious I really was in following Christ.

After the service on that first Sunday visit, a couple of the deacons talked with me. When one of them asked if I planned to return the following week, I replied that I did not know, and that I would have to talk it over with my wife, who was across the room, talking with their wives. I sensed that my response did not get much traction with them, and so I explained,

"And then, I do have to work every third Sunday, since I'm on a one-day-on, two-day-off schedule."

One of them was a paramedic himself, a veteran with many years in the field. He answered,

"Well, you can get trades, or use vacation time, or even give away the hours. God will work it out for you to make it to a place where you can really grow, Ken. Don't you think he can replace whatever income you might feel like you're losing to be a disciple, Ken? He really cares that much about you and your growth. It's a matter of what you value most in life. This obviously seems to be an opportunity that God has presented to you to really grow in his calling on your life to follow him and demonstrate trust in him."

"Uh, well," I stammered, "as a rookie, I kind of don't want to make waves by taking time off work right away. I have only been on the job for a couple of months."

The other deacon said nothing for a few moments, and then thoughtfully replied,

"Right, Ken. Well, we would not ask anything of you that Jesus did not ask of his own disciples."

I was hooked.

Although I did not become aware of the concept of *totalism* for many years, when I read about it for the first time, there was not the slightest doubt that it described me at that time of my life with absolute precision. I was a religious totalist.

Totalism describes the ideological mindset behind its political (and probably more familiar) application, *totalitarianism*. A totalitarian regime or government is one that controls and demands the complete subjection, loyalty, and obedience of every citizen that belongs to it. It achieves that subjection by forcing every expression of culture to bow to its authority. Nothing exists independent of the demands, requirements, and oversight of the totalitarian regime: the political system, arts and entertainment industries, athletic organizations, educational system from preschool through university, military and police system, healthcare, prisons, transportation, and agricultural and industrial systems. Everything is under the control of the totalitarian state. Totalism is the underlying philosophy of totalism. Totalism does not simply demand adherence to the rules and demands of the authority—it demands its subjects adopt the belief system of the authority. Totalism is the domination of the thinking, not simply the behavior, of a person.[3] Abusive churches and cults do not simply control people's behaviors. After all, we live in a relatively free country, where citizens are granted the rights of life, liberty, and the pursuit of happiness. No, such churches, with their totalist ideologies, are out to change the thinking of members, largely through restricting members' access to truth through lying, manipulation, and secrecy of motives. As the beliefs of members change, their behaviors change, too, according to the new beliefs. Totalism works from the inside out to control its victims. And as cults and coercive groups especially in the West have demonstrated, when a person's thinking is

3. See Lifton, *Thought Reform and the Psychology of Totalism*; Martin, *Heresy of Mind Control*; and the abstract by Lifton, "Cult Formation."

controlled there is no need for physical constraint, for the person actually chooses to be controlled.

I was a religious totalist in that I truly believed that every aspect of my life (behavior, personality, habits, tastes, etc.) should comply with the demands of my new discipline—the Christian faith. Although I could not see it at the time, I was simply waiting for a totalist Christian leader to come along who would seek to control every aspect of my life and point out all of the areas that I had been holding out on God. There is an abusive leader at the end of every totalist organization. And my totalist tendencies made me low-hanging fruit for the narcissistic, totalist pastor who preached that day about the evils of leaving the place God has brought you—even if that place is a little ranch-style house with twenty-five people meeting in its living room, and deacons who spiritually bully you after the service.

And, as far as I could determine, God *had* brought me to that living room that day. If I had known then what I know today of what that little living-room church would become to me—and what it would do to me, and to my marriage and children—I would have thrown my folding chair through the front window, grabbed my wife, and crawled out over the shards of glass. Instead, I went home and pulled out an employee phone list and prayed that God would find me a paramedic who might be willing to trade a shift so I could attend church the next Sunday.

Chapter 5

Inside the Abusive Church

ARE THERE SPECIFIC SIGNS that a church is abusive or cultlike? Are there any solid conditions that we can confidently say are unhealthy and indicative of abuse? Do the members all dress alike? Do they give all of their money to the church? Is the preacher at an abusive church charismatic, confident, and a bit flamboyant? Is he creepy? Can they accidentally join an abusive church, without realizing what they're doing? How can current or potential members be sure they are dealing with an abusive church, and not simply a church with beliefs and practices that they don't agree with? These are some of the questions you might have as you consider whether a church seems to be unhealthy and abusive.

I believe there are seven indicators of spiritually abusive churches. These indicators may all be present, or only some of them, and they will probably be represented in differing levels of intensity. But from the first instances of exposure to an abusive church, with its subtle deceptions and misinformation, to the growing fear of displeasing leaders, to the traumatic experience in leaving the church, I have found most of these indicators present in every abusive church I have become aware of: deception; isolation; elitism; fear; mandated disclosure; and trauma upon leaving the church.

Deception: What Members Receive
Is Not What They Were Promised

Members of abusive churches do not receive what they were promised when they were encouraged to join. Abusive churches do not share their full stories or agendas with those they seek to recruit. They do not come and say,

> Hey, we're the only *true* church in this town. All of the other churches are phonies and spineless, uncommitted groups of people playing at religion. We, on the other hand, are the real deal.

That would be pretty off-putting to new members or first-time visitors.

Instead, abusive churches simply present their own teachings and truth claims as the only acceptable way to believe, period. Indeed, although it's unstated and unacknowledged, the first (devastating) commitment that members make to an abusive church is that they will allow the church to be their greatest authority on the determination of truth. They'll listen to the leaders first to determine what truth is. Soon, their reliance on the abusive church for truth will become fiercely exclusive. There simply will be no outside source of information that they trust. Once they believe that the church (through its leaders and members) is the final source of truth, they begin to base their decision-making on what they are told by the abusive church, and they become controlled by the church.

A common way that members of abusive churches are deceived is when they are promised the spiritual benefits they will experience as they participate in church life will be commensurate with the degree of commitment they make to the church. In the initial stages, they may hear extravagant claims and assertions regarding the group's success and resources.

I joined an abusive church because I was told that the church possessed the structure and academic opportunities that would prepare me for vocational ministry. Its pastors even boasted that they were far more qualified than any seminary to train pastors, and they discouraged me from pursuing formal seminary studies. They were intelligent, articulate, and confident; and they seemed interested in me and supportive of my career goals. So I listened to them, and they convinced me (for a while) to avoid formal studies and instead join their church as a means of training for the pastorate. Led by my desire for spiritual growth and my (obvious) ambition to be in vocational ministry, I was easily recruited. But I did not come even remotely close to experiencing the career training and opportunities I had been promised when I joined the church.

Many people are also manipulated into joining by the promise of close friendships within a Christian, healthy community. Everyone wants to be valued, respected, and viewed with affection and warmth by friends and family alike. A fellow survivor told me,

> I joined that church simply because I thought I would be loved and valued for who I am, just like the Bible says. Instead, I was only noticed and valued when I was doing well—keeping the rules and expectations of the church. I guess what it boils down to is that they promised me, at the beginning, that I would be loved, unconditionally. But what I received was the most conditional love that is humanly possible.

The particular claims and promises made to new members are varied and tailored to their desires and hopes. Often, these expectations are shared with the new members by other, more tenured members who themselves are still living in the hope of experiencing what *they* had been promised. But in the end, the members learn that the kindness and acceptance they seek is conditioned upon their continued devotion to the church and particularly, its pastor. They simply do not experience what was promised.

To repeat: People do not *join* abusive churches. They are *recruited* into churches that make wonderful, personally tailored promises to them of a blessed, healthy, and satisfying social and spiritual life. They are not told of the demands that will be made on them, the social pressures they will live under, the challenges that will follow. They are never encouraged to speak with former members, to understand the experiences and perspectives of people who have decided not to attend the church. They are never let in on the finances of the church.[1] They are never told beforehand of the burdensome expectations and demands that will be placed on their time, their outside relationships, their marriages, and their parenting practices. Instead, they are promised great gains in all these areas—if only they will take the plunge, count the cost, commit, follow the Master, and so on.

And therein is the deceit: For, in the abusive church, members will never receive what is promised, no matter how much blood and sweat they lose to gain it.

Loss: The Abusive Church Demands More— of Everything

Members' resources will increasingly flow from *the members* into *the abusive church.* Abusive churches do not exist to enrich the lives of their members. Rather, they enrich the lives of their leaders, who demand the unfailing loyalty, obedience, and singular attachment of each member—often expressed in that member handing over increasing amounts of personal resources.

The most obvious resource that comes to mind is money. Abusive churches pressure their members to contribute amounts that are excessive and damaging to their financial, material health. Often, leaders solicit extra financial support for what they may refer to as *special* needs, gifts, and opportunities that relate to the mission of the church.

For instance, in one Dallas, Texas, church, in addition to its required tithe of 10 percent of its members' incomes, an additional "asset tithe," in which 10 percent of the value of each member's net worth (stocks, bonds, real estate, cars, bank accounts, and belongings) were required of the members. Thereafter, a "First Fruits" tithe policy was instituted, in which each member submitted a

---

1. In a podcast relating to cults, therapist Daniel Shaw made a memorable statement: "In cults, there are two sets of books; the one that they show everyone, and the one that tells what is really going on."

personal budget to the pastor, who then determined the amount of money each was to hand over to the church.[2]

In my abusive church, our pastor got the creative idea that for his thirty-eighth birthday the church should give him a birthday gift of $100 for each year of his life. Of course, he wasn't going to just come out and announce his plan—he had his sister, the church secretary, announced it to church members. And the plan (we survivors now wryly remember it as "the Birthday Tax") worked for a couple of years, making the pastor's birthday a very lucrative time—for him. It was an embarrassing, costly, burdensome time for the barely three dozen members of his church.

A friend of mine recounted the slide into financial crisis that she and her family faced as they were pressured to give increasing amounts of money in support of their abusive church:

> There was a very clear, overt demand to give. As the main breadwinner in my household and one of the "larger salaries" in the church, I was expected to support my mother-in-law [a fellow member of the church] financially as well as provide a large tithe each month. The support of my mother-in-law was so that she would not be a "financial burden" to the church community. My husband was not working and we were often behind in rent and utilities. Nevertheless, that didn't matter as long as the pastor was supported. I was discouraged from contributing to my company's 401k plan—that would take money away, and we were encouraged to expand exemptions on taxes so that more money came in. I had an opportunity to take on a part-time job in my previous career of journalism. This was met with hostility and mistrust and I was informed that it was God's will that I stay in my current job.

How do abusive churches get away with such ridiculous, low-brow methods and justifications for stealing their members' precious dollars? They usually work up to such robberies by establishing a powerful influence over each member's most precious,

2. Glenna Whitley, "The Cult of Ole," *Dallas Observer*, September 17, 2016, http://www.dallasobserver.com/news/the-cult-of-ole-6406297.

irreplaceable treasure—time. Presented with what is often an exhausting, dizzying array of activities, new members are expected to attend most, if not all, of the ministries and activities offered at the church. Members may be told they are *invited*, but they understand that they are really *expected* to attend midweek services and studies, early morning prayer meetings, classes for training in evangelism, or other faith-related activities. There may also be specialized ministries, outreach programs, conferences, and unique training or service-oriented events. As the members invest more of their time, more of their lives become deeply, personally invested in the abusive church. They run out of resources to do anything else with their lives, for they have given over their resources to enrich the life of the church and its leaders.

The continued drain on the resources of members can be measured not solely by the money that they give *over* to the church, but also through the opportunities for personal, material, and vocational gain that they give *up* for the church.

Abusive churches often rob young marriages and parents of time with their family. The early years of a marriage and family are often marked by lots of bills and diapers, and not much money. But one resource that is critical for the newly married, and for young families, is time. And time is what the abusive church demands of the younger couples and families. Researcher Dale Enroth notes that abusive churches often target younger, less established families for recruitment:

> Such [abusive] churches often target young couples during the crucial childbearing years. As a result, the energy needed by these young couples for legitimate family interaction is siphoned off into a high intensity cause. Family obligations are sacrificed, and children's developmental needs are neglected.[3]

Abusive churches indirectly take their members' resources by discouraging them from pursuing professional and personal goals—particularly when pursuing those goals deflects resources

3. Enroth, "Dysfunctional Churches."

(and possibly members' attendance) away from the church. The International Church of Christ (ICC) is infamous for its aggressive college-campus recruitment of students, and the subsequent counseling of those students to either diminish their class load or drop out of college altogether. The reason? So that they are more available to serve and participate in the activities of the church.

My friend Don left a successful medical practice to be more available to his church:

> The demands of the church led to me abandoning my previous career for a career as a vocational disciple-maker. Because the vision I bought into was sold to me by a fraud, when I finally left the church, I found myself starting at square one in my mid-forties. (personal communication)

I deeply regret inviting a friend that I served with in the US Army to my abusive church. He was a professional helicopter pilot and former officer in the Army. Once he became a member of the church, he was pressured by its leaders to give up his aviation career in order to remain in the area, all to be more available for ministry. He was then cajoled into taking a job as a field laborer at a local tree farm, at a severe reduction of his pay, all the while being told by our church leaders that he was making a grand choice by remaining in a place where he could really grow in his faith. (Wherever he is today—I hope he is well—and flying!)

One survivor told me of the effect on his marriage of his wife quitting her job in nursing to become a paid pastoral assistant—paid on a *quid pro quo* basis, whereby the family lived in a church-sponsored communal home with a reduction of their monthly rent:

> The biggest loss was that of my wife's time. She became the "full-time assistant" to the leader, giving up the possibility of part- or full-time nursing wages, for a rent reduction benefit of $600/month, which was of course far less than minimum wage. I was expected to be grateful for all the supposed benefits flowing to us from this arrangement. This made it impossible to deal with debts,

took priority over family life, and in the end, contributed to the failure of the marriage. (personal communication)

Naturally, much attention is drawn to the gross excesses of modern televangelists and megachurch pastors, with their opulent homes, fleets of expensive cars, collections of vacation homes, and private jets. But in my experience, the resources that the abusive pastor extracts from the members of his church serve a much more sinister end: they signify the members' all-in attachment to the pastor. Social psychologist Alexandra Stein's recent work *Terror, Love, and Brainwashing: Attachment in Cults and Authoritarian Systems* presents the totalist leader (for this discussion, the abusive, narcissistic pastor) is more driven by the need for undiluted attachment from members than by the desire for gain of material and resources. She writes,

> The need to control others as a means of guaranteeing attachment is the one consistent feature of cult leaders— not all of them seek to increase wealth as a result of their domination of followers. But of course, once a leader has succeeded in controlling group members' attachment to him or herself, then these other benefits can accrue as well.[4]

Take over their lives, and the money (and everything else) will follow.

Isolation: "No Need for Anybody Else . . . You've Got Us Now!"

Abusive churches discourage their members from forming and maintaining healthy relationships with nonmembers, unless the nonmembers are candidates for recruitment into the church. Although it is rarely expressed as a *rule* to be followed, abusive churches often isolate their members from their (nonmember) families and friends. The family, friends, and coworkers of the member are either subtly or openly held in a negative light, and their significance to the

---

4. Stein, *Terror, Love & Brainwashing*, 113–14.

member is disregarded, if not outright challenged. Members may be led to believe that those who are not members of the church are truly substandard people who are unworthy of time, affection, and attention. Unless there seems a likelihood of them being recruited into the church, family and friends are gradually pushed to the edges of members' thoughts and concerns. Members may begin to believe that their former friends, their family, and their coworkers are antagonists, standing in the way of the member's continued spiritual growth and availability to the church. The questions, concerns, and confusion regarding the fanatical commitment the member has made to the church, and its powerful hold over him, are perceived by the member as unfair, intrusive, critical, nagging, and unenlightened.

"My commitment is to Jesus," or "My commitment is to the Great Commission—not to a church," members will respond. But they soon learn that the commitment truly *is* to the church—to that specific church, of which they are members.

That's why I had it out with my dad one day regarding my decision to sell a house. Sharon and I sold our first house and purchased one of lesser quality and value to live closer to the church community, and to be available for its ministries and activities. We also hoped to have a positive impact on the poorer, lower-class neighborhood we moved into. (Our new neighbors were not impressed, I'm afraid.) The moving decision didn't sit well with our folks. And then, just to add more crazy to the mix, a couple of years later we sold that home when we were offered the *opportunity* (that's the word we used to describe obligation and pressure) to move into a large home, shared by the senior pastor and several other church members, for more intense, daily discipleship training. We decided to move into this expansive, rented house with our two preschool-aged daughters, renting two bedrooms for our family of four, and sharing the rest of the house with the pastor and his wife, two other families, and several single adults. What could go wrong?

My father was not impressed by our zeal. When we put our home on the market (we ended up selling it at a loss), he stopped by one day to confront my rash behavior, and to try to talk sense into me. He expressed his heartfelt concern for the type of home and lifestyle that our choices would most likely create for his granddaughters, and he questioned the wisdom of our decision to abandon home ownership to become renters, not even of our own house, but of rooms in a rented house:

> What about the kids, Kenny? What about their lives? What about the home they'll grow up in? What about your marriage? What about your future, your reputation, Kenny? Have you really thought about this, son? What are you doing?

I was incensed:

> Dad, I'm *doing* something here, not just living like everyone else, trying to get ahead, get rich, and save my pennies! I want to *count* for something more than just owning my own home. I want this chance to grow deeper in my faith, to be discipled! I'm training to be a pastor. This is how I'm doing it, and it's none of your business to come to *my* house and criticize me! You should be proud of me, that I'm making a choice here to follow Jesus more closely. Instead, you come here to criticize me. I can't believe it! And you say you are a Christian!

Not one of my finer moments in my relationship with my dad.

But the time for Dad and me to have such a conversation was long past. I'd already made the decision, years earlier, to submit myself to the direction and counsel of my pastor. I now operated from a completely different set of beliefs and values about life, meaning, and purpose than what I had grown up with. I believed I was very different from my extended family, and we could no longer be close. I had new friends; friends who understood me, and could relate to my life experience. Those friends were my fellow church members. I naturally began to pull away from my family and (lifelong) friends.

And so we did it. We moved into the large, rented house atop a mountain, overlooking the city of Portland. I cannot recall a single time when I felt the desire or the freedom to invite anyone from my family over for a visit, though they lived only a couple of miles away. I recall a nagging feeling, deep in my gut, that I was not acting like much of a Christian—rejecting my folks, discounting their concerns for me and my family, withdrawing from all of them, and disregarding their concerns for the environment in which I was raising my daughters. But they'd been pushed to such a far back burner in my life, it hardly seemed possible to even let them into the decision, let alone value their input. I had a new family now, I told myself, as I had been told by the church.

Parents, siblings, and in-laws often note that their loved one who belongs to an abusive church no longer seems to enjoy, desire, or value activities that are the bedrock of family life. Birthdays, anniversaries, holidays, reunions, recreational activities, just hanging out together over a cup of coffee or a beer—the member no longer values these times. In truth, he no longer has time for them; and over time, his participation is less and less frequent. Friends and family members get the point and may simply stop inviting him to events and gatherings. The withdrawal of invitations becomes a sadly self-fulfilling act: The member is confirmed in the idea that he was never loved or valued anyway and is better off with the abusive church than he ever was with family and friends.

That is the *physical* part—the member being present in body. But even when he does attend family activities, he is increasingly not there in *spirit*—his personality has changed. He is now very serious about most things and has become flat, tense, and distant. His family is at first confused, then hurt, and then annoyed. They report,

> He used to be the life of the party, He was fun to be around and seemed to enjoy himself so much. Now, he seems repressed, stilted, boring, and sad. The only time he really lights up around family is when the conversation has turned (usually, turned by him!) to religion. He could go on and on and on (and he does!) about it—and even more so, about how crummy *our* religion is compared to his new religion, how *dead* our church is compared to how *alive* his church is, how our pastor is so dull, so lukewarm, but his, of course, may as well

be the thirteenth apostle! He obviously thinks we are not "saved," or, at least, not as "serious about Jesus" as he is, and he does not hide his condescending attitude very well.

Good grief! Last Christmas he asked if we took notes of our pastor's sermons! He knew we don't take notes. Never have. He just wanted to make the point that *he* takes notes of his pastor's sermons. Ugh. We stopped wanting him around at many of our family events because he has become so judgmental and arrogant. Who is this religious zombie that has inhabited our son's body? Where is *our* boy?!

And that is the crux of the issue, really. *Their boy* is no longer *their boy*.

In time, his family and friends get used to the new reality, and they accept his membership in the group. Over the years, babies are born, engagements announced, anniversaries and graduations celebrated, illnesses faced, and deaths grieved, all with the understanding that the beloved member of the abusive church will not be there—or, at best, will not be *all* there.

You might be wondering, *Why would a church ever want to cut its members off from their families and friends? Does that go against the basic idea of the church growing?* And you would be completely correct in wondering that.

Every abusive church is a communal expression and product of the dysfunction and narcissism of an abusive pastor—even if the pastor has died and others have taken his place. Sometimes the isolation is just a result of a bad pastor being jealous of his members expressing affection or value for anyone other than himself, or his church. But the very processes of thought reform that occur in abusive churches also depend on isolation of members from contrary ideas and perspectives that threaten the church's teachings, policies, and behaviors. Leaders of such churches simply do not want members to hear any other views, and they certainly do not want them to critically evaluate what they're being told in the church. Thought reform is the subversion and malevolent manipulation of how a person *thinks*. So abusive, thought-reforming churches put a lot of effort into changing the way their members think about people who are outside the church—even if those people are the family members, old friends, Army buddies, and coworkers who used to be the best friends the member had.

"Who needs those friends? You've got us."

"Who needs your family? *We're* your family now!"

Elitism: "It's Hard to Be Humble When You're Simply So Great"

Abusive churches believe they are better than all others, and they view other churches with disdain. Abusive churches are very impressed with themselves and live in the thick, intoxicating fog of elitism. From the pulpit to the parking lot, the message swirls through the congregation that there is simply no church quite like *this* church. Fostering an elitist environment is a critical part of gaining the loyalty and trust of the church's members. Elitism serves not only to give the member assurance that he has indeed chosen the *right* church for himself, but also that his church is better than any of the other churches he might have chosen to join. He may even be told that it was certainly an act of a providence that he ended up in his church, and he would be appalled by the very thought that he was actually recruited into the church. And once he has committed himself to what he believes is the most faithful, most effective, and most *serious* church in the neighborhood, he must continually be reminded of the superior quality of his church—despite his growing experience of evidence to contrary!

The abusive church convinces members that its teachings, traditions, and practices are not only faithful to the Bible and the Christian faith, but are the *most faithful* to those things than any other church in the area. A common mark of high-demand, abusive churches is their bold-faced efforts to recruit new members to their churches from neighboring ones. And why not? Bully pastors proclaim their churches superior, and other churches as "backslidden," "compromised," or "lukewarm." These pastors see these efforts of convincing others to abandon their churches as a rescue mission.

But how can a person be snatched away from his church, perhaps one that he has belonged to for many years? The strategy is simple. Argue that his faith *demands* he leave his church if he finds a better church, and present the demand in reasonable terms, ones that appeal to values he already holds. Point out the supposed spiritual deficiencies in the spiritual life of a potential recruit:

> "So, how is your study discipline going? Are you spending regular time in the word?"

> "Does your church train you in how to share your faith?"

> "Is your church offering any kind of discipleship? Are you growing in your ability to encourage and train a younger believer in his faith?"

> "Are you *really* getting closer to people in the church—not just seeing them on Sundays, but *doing* life together all week long?"

> "Is your church growing much? I mean *really growing*—not just bodies in the pews. Is the Spirit powerfully present there?"

> "Do you believe God's will for your life is to grow in your faith? If you found a place where you could grow more in your faith than you are growing now, do you think it would be worth checking out? Maybe God is leading you to do that."

Of *course*, all Christians want to grow deeper and mature in their faith, to some degree. Of *course*, they feel a need to grow more. Of *course*, they would like to help out newer Christians, and receive encouragement and help in their own spiritual lives. No Christian (with a sane assessment of themselves!) would ever claim to have it all together, and to be beyond the need for growth and improvement.

Once the lackluster nature of the potential recruits' respective churches is established, and their spiritual deficiencies are ever-so-gently exposed, then comes the invitation:

> Well, my church *does* offer spiritual mentoring—to everyone. And we study the Bible very seriously—a lot! Before I joined my church, I was a pretty self-satisfied, lukewarm believer. I never witnessed to anyone. I didn't study the Bible. To tell the truth, I usually just slept in on Sundays. I wasn't being challenged at all. Now, I'm a part of great group of people who are *really doing* Christianity—not just talking about it. Finally, I've got a church family that *truly cares* about me and is committed to me, no matter what. Why don't you visit this Sunday and see what you think?

The recruiter need only pick and poke around at the spiritual life of the Christian being recruited, and once a vulnerable, lackluster area of faith is identified (i.e., relationships, marriage, parenting, job, Bible study, sharing the gospel, having friends, finding meaning in the church), contrast the failure of his church in providing such growth with the raving success of the recruiter's church. The approach is especially effective with those Christians who are dissatisfied, anxious, guilt-ridden, and not experiencing joy, freedom, growth, and other positive dynamics in their own churches. It's really what worked to get me and my wife through the doors of the church that we joined, convinced that we'd finally found that one, right church for us—the better church.

Abusive pastors are not shy to point out the supposed flaws of their neighboring churches—noting supposed doctrinal deficiencies, spiritual tepidness, cold-faith, dead orthodoxy, and any other seeming vulnerabilities. The pastor of my abusive church encouraged the single members of our church to attend the midweek services of other local churches in our city. I thought it strange that he would do so, given that he was generally critical and distant from other churches and pastors, and often spoke ill of them from the pulpit. Years later, I learned of the reason behind his encouragement: After attending the midweek services of other churches, our members would gather at the pastor's home and report to him all of the flaws and inconsistencies that they had found in the churches they'd visited. The pastor loved to hear other churches being criticized, while he himself was complimented and affirmed as being superior to them all!

The elitism that permeates life in an abusive church has no correspondence to reality, and smacks of the very hyper-religiousness and pride condemned in the Bible. But it does accomplish its goal of solidifying members' confidence, not only that they have chosen the right church to belong to, but also (as they are often told) that God himself brought them there. It is an intoxicating confidence, dulling the member's sensitivity to the pressure, manipulation, and overweening control that the church has laid on his shoulders.

Fear: Dread of Displeasing Leaders

Members of abusive churches are afraid of displeasing their leaders. Abusive churches are spiritual communities of fear. This fear is a mechanism of control, for members are increasingly motivated, not by a *desire to please* their abusive pastors, but by the *fear of displeasing* them. A complex system of rewards and punishments is gradually applied to the life of the member, making him vulnerable to manipulation. As my wife and I became embedded within our church and increasingly identified with its pastor, I became vulnerable to his control in what seemed every area of my life. I realized that he had gained tremendous power and influence in the most important relationships in my life—those with my wife and my children. He could also turn my closest friends in the church against me, belittle me before the congregation, question the sincerity of my faith, and discourage people from becoming friends with me. He could institute a dozen different types of shunning against me—without me even knowing I was being shunned until I sensed the coolness and withdrawal of friends. He could suggest to my children that I was a substandard father. He could mention to my wife that he had noticed my lack of attention to her, and that I did not seem to love her as much as she loved me. He could remove me from valued positions of responsibility in the church and betray private issues of sin and confession that I had shared with him. He could chip away at my self-esteem, confidence, and sense of worth.

How did I know he could inflict that kind of punishment on me? Simply because in each of those areas that is precisely what he did.

Take shunning, for example. The power to invoke the shunning of a member by his or her fellow church members is perhaps the greatest power the abusive pastor possesses. When a person has been indoctrinated and assimilated into the abusive church, he has abandoned his outside friendships, alienated his extended family, and often has pulled away from healthy, satisfying relationships with coworkers and neighbors. His spouse and children likely are also members of his church. His (new) best friends are in the church, and his spiritual mentors are, of course, in the church. In short, he belongs to a world in which all his friends and family are members of the same abusive system, are just as pliable as he, and, should they fall afoul of the pastor and leaders of the church, are just as likely to reject as to be rejected.

The fear of displeasing the abusive pastor makes members say things they don't believe and do things they don't desire to do. But to refuse his guidance and directives brings his displeasure, so church members in the grips of such abuse go out of their way to demonstrate the exclusive loyalty and submission expected by their leader. It is not surprising that living in such a state of fear creates great anxiety and fear in these members of abusive churches, despite the outer, superficial appearance that they are quite happy and satisfied.

Scratch gently on the confident, smooth surface of someone who is being spiritually abused, and you'll find a frightened person beneath.

Disclosure: Confession as a Price of Membership

Abusive churches require indiscriminate, intrusive confession from members. Harmful churches tend to coerce confessions of sin and failure out of their members. In this delicate, precious area of members' souls, the deepest wounds are inflicted and often are the wounds that take the longest to heal.

Confession is the acknowledgment of sin and failure. The word *confess*, translated in the original, Greek language that the New Testament was written in, is *homologeo*—literally, *to speak the same*. When I confess a sin, it means that I have agreed with my faith, as I best understand it, that my behavior was wrong. In a sense, confession is simply speaking the truth to oneself, to God, and to anyone else one chooses to share with. Confession is a healthy part of the Christian life and is needed daily. Indeed, no serious approach to spiritual growth and maturation leaves out the issue of confession as a means of personal growth and spiritual health. The Bible promises Christians that, when they confess their sins to God, he hears them, forgives them, and even takes their confession as an invitation to lead them to better behavior and living in the future (1 John 1:9). Confession is not a quick route to spiritual maturity or wisdom, but as an acquired habit of life it becomes a path that leads to those things.

Of course, abusive churches don't see it that way.

In the church that abuses, the confession of sin (whether actual or imagined) is wrung out of members as a means of gaining emotional control over them. Such coerced confession strengthens the control that abusive pastors hold over church members. Not content to simply hear members' confession of their sins, abusive leaders proceed to extract their innermost thoughts and feelings, which violates what is often members' last safe place: their conscience. This practice has three damaging effects on the life of the church: it empowers the abusive pastor, it damages the member, and it weakens relationships among fellow members of the congregation.

Forced confession introduces a mythical perception of abusive leaders, creating the appearance that such leaders possess a deeper level of insight and wisdom beyond that of the groups' members. Simply suggesting to members that there is "something there to confess" is unsettling to them, for almost everyone has *something* they can find that is deficient in their faith and in need of addressing.

"Surely there is *some* sin, *some* secret, *some* desire or temptation that is there, that should be 'opened up' for healing," such leaders say, implying that they already know what that sin is.

In my former church, for instance, the senior pastor routinely confronted his members in smaller group settings with the accusation that they were clinging to a "secret agenda" for their lives, some plan or intention that involved them leaving his church, harboring resentment or anger against him, or secretly saving up money. He referred to such seditious desires and goals as members' "Plan B"—the secret plans they clung to and nurtured as an escape from what he claimed was the true way at his church, the life of following God. Of course, there were plenty of Plan Bs among his followers—but they were all plans for escaping him and his abusive church! There were evenings when he harangued small groups of church members for hours upon hours—attempting to unearth secret resentments and jealousies—all related to him. It soon became apparent that no answer or confession could assure him of our loyalty to both him and his ministry. But his goal was not to uncover anything of what any of us felt or thought. It was more sinister: to break the wills of the members through violating their most intimate, private thoughts. Once broken, repentant, apologetic members were graciously forgiven by the pastor, and the group quickly followed and affirmed affection for the humbled, broken individuals. The sessions ended in exhaustion, tears, and hugging, an experience Lifton called "an orgiastic sense of oneness."[5] We were trauma-bonding, gaining a deep sense of closeness and identification with one another through having faced ongoing cycles of emotional punishment, confession, breaking, and reward.

5. Lifton, *Thought Reform*, 426.

Naturally, coerced confession inflicts horrible damage on the lives of the members of the abusive church, leaving deep, indelible scars.[6] Lifton refers to this self-revealing, self-condemning ritual as the *cult of confession*. In their earliest experiences of confession in the church, members may initially find the coerced, indiscriminate bearing of their souls to be agreeable and even beneficial. Through confession, they may find personal purification from sin, or powerful identification with the church membership. They may experience acceptance and the perception of forgiveness of their sins. They may even find temporary relief from the free-floating sense of guilt and shame that we often carry through life.

But whatever positive experiences of confession that a member may have found soon are exposed for their conditional nature. The member will experience acceptance and supposed understanding as he continues to confess, ever more deeply and intimately, his sin and failures. And unlike healthy confession, the coerced confession of the abusive church leaves its members vulnerable, unprotected, and with the lasting wounds of emotional violation.

Coerced confession also carries a surprising irony, producing the exact opposite of its intended goal. Lifton writes, "The cult of confession has effects quite the reverse of its ideal of total exposure: rather than eliminating personal secrets, it increases and intensifies them."[7] As confession in the abusive church becomes increasingly a macabre, dramatic performance to members, they lose the ability to truly confess what they genuinely believe to *be* sin. Instead, they share what they think will *sound* like sin. Members become the very persons that their confession of sin was supposed to ensure they would *not* become, hypocrites. In addition, as they routinely share their innermost secrets along with fabricated sins and wrongs, they lose clarity on who they really are, and on what they have really done, thought, or said. They lose the ability to form and maintain genuinely close relationships. Their secrets, normally shared only with great care and circumspection with

6. Lifton, *Thought Reform*, 426.

7. Lifton, *Thought Reform*, 426.

their closest, most intimate friends, may become common fare in the church. And even confession of the deepest sins does not satisfy, for the requirement is always the same—continued confession and self-exposure.

Coerced confession is a violation of the trust, courtesy, and acceptance that should mark a healthy congregation. When members tolerate confession used as a tool against their fellow members, they act as unwitting assistants to the abusive leader. They also become desensitized to the mistreatment of their fellow members. A fellow survivor described her experience of coerced confession to me, and her pastor's cruel enjoyment of making his members squirm:

> Our narcissistic pastor had no conscience whatsoever. He enjoyed the process of traumatizing people. It was easy to see the gratification he derived from making people grovel. There was incredible pressure to join him in the torment. It sometimes felt as though we were picking up stones to throw at our friends. The difference was that we did have consciences. We felt sick inside. We were anxious for the conflict to be resolved so we could reassure our friends. Unfortunately, as time went on, our consciences became impaired, and we rarely gave reassurance or support to fellow members, no matter how badly they were treated.

Coerced confession creates a false, *non*-community, in which the unconditional acceptance and love inherently promised to members upon joining is subtly replaced with a conditional acceptance—one that depends on members enduring emotional humiliation to maintain their sense of belongingness in the group. When confession is perverted in this way, and admissions of sin, failure, and unworthiness are emphasized more than forgiveness, grace, and the genuine joy of being accepted by God, then the church becomes a cult of confession.

Trauma: Leaving Is Painful and Costly

Abusive churches use fear, obstacles and punishments to prevent members from leaving. When I envisioned a life away from the abusive church, I realized that I had been living in a trap. And as I (very privately) considered leaving, I began to feel the pressure, obstacles, and threats that were designed by our church leaders to force me to stay.

It's only when we want to leave the theater that we look for the exit doors. And when we notice with alarm that the doors have been locked on the inside, we realize the person with the keys to the theater does not want us to leave the show. Likewise, when members think of leaving the church, its trap-like nature becomes soberingly evident.

An effective trap has three necessary aspects: It must present some sort of bait to attract its prey, it must be relatively easy to enter to get the bait, and it must be either impossible (or excruciatingly painful) to escape from. Likewise, abusive churches offer the bait of supposed unconditional love in the context of a Christian community, they are easy to enter into—often through the invitation of a trusted friend or family member, and they are often very painful and troublesome to leave.

The trauma of leaving an abusive church begins before members actually walk out the door, and usually continues long after they have been free of the church. Active members are besieged with threats of the doom, the loss, and the divine disfavor that awaits those who dare to leave the church. And they truly will experience trauma when they finally do leave. It is often while they are still in the church that members come to understand very clearly how difficult leaving might be. They may hear warnings about the foolishness of leaving, the likelihood of divine displeasure dogging them for the rest of their days, the certainty of personal catastrophe, and the loss of their friends.[8] They may be told

8. More than one former member of the abusive church I left has related to me that the current members were told that I hated them. One survivor left the church and called me. He was tentative and meek, having been told that I would certainly have no time for "defectors" and "washed out" Christians such

that their marriage won't survive, or that their children might get sick or may well end up as juvenile delinquents.[9] (For a while in my abusive church, I believed my daughters would suffer greatly should I leave the church, and for a period of time I was unsure if my wife would even leave with me.) These types of threats and fears often lead members to remain in the church long after they have decided they want to leave it.

Abusive pastors often mock and deride members who have left the church. Any departure from the church to pursue secular career or academic goals is often demeaned and criticized. Members are treated as if such goals are unworthy of followers of Jesus Christ, and that all faithful Christians should be prioritizing the pursuit of either professional ministry or simply lives and careers that afford the most hours of the week to be spent proselytizing for the church, and supporting its ministries.

Warnings are couched in mean-spirited criticism of those who already have left the church:

"Heidi left Jesus to overfocus on her family instead of following Jesus."

"Drake wants the American Dream more than Jesus, so he left Jesus."

"Robert would rather make money than make disciples."

"Karl wants to spend more time fishing than worshiping God."

"Jim struggled with spiritual authority and decided to go it alone. He wants his own church, so he can be in charge."

"Susan would rather party than follow the Lord."

---

as he was. Nothing could be further from the truth; I miss my old friends who remain in the church, and I pray for them to come to their better senses and escape the prison they've chosen to live in!

9. Some churches even allow the marriages of members to dissolve, encouraging a spouse who wishes to remain in the church to reject the spouse who wants to leave, or to make the continuance of the marriage conditioned on the spouse deciding to remain in the church.

Low-brow, petty words. But the reason for the nastiness is not simply to express disdain for the member who left. Its purpose is to make an impact on those who remain. Cutting down those who leave an abusive church communicates to those members who remain that, should they leave the church, they too will be spoken and thought of in such disparaging and disrespectful ways—and the put-downs and derision will come from the lips of those whom they considered their friends in the church. This keeps many abused people in abusive churches for years; for despite the abuse and absurdity of life in an abusive church, the members *are* your closest friends, after all. This is how the trauma involved in leaving the abusive church begins before members even walk out the door.

Many members who leave abusive churches continue to experience trauma from their experiences for months and years afterward. My wife and I walked out of the home that we shared with several other church members to the harsh, berating yells of the associate pastor—a memory that we will certainly never forget! Others in our church, having displeased the senior pastor through some supposed offense, were immediately evicted from church-established homes where they had lived, sometimes for years. Some found their belongings had been boxed up and left on the front porch—they were not welcome to even enter the house. I recall the pastor telling one departing member of the church,

"You're probably not even saved, and you're going to die alone in a nursing home."

Again, these insulting, disrespectful behaviors on the part of the leaders and members of the abusive church were twofold in their intent: they punished the exiting members, and they warned the remaining members exactly how they would be treated, should they leave the church. The depth of emotional-psychological pain inflicted in such treatment makes recovery from the abusive church much more difficult and extended.

Of even greater intensity is the trauma experienced by those children who are born into or raised in the abusive church and then decide to leave it as teens or as adults. In my experience, the very least effect of their decision to exit results in a general discomfort and coolness from their parents, and the most extreme result is total rejection of the child by the parent. Years after my departure, I heard the stories of several former members of my church who had run away from the church-led homes in which they'd been raised. Out of fear, and the certainty of rejection and conflict, they did not discuss their decision to leave, even with their parents. Of those (now) young adults that I am friends with who grew up in my church, none were pursued or contacted by their parents after running away. This is the model that children in such churches grow up observing, fearing, and choosing—rather than continuing in the impossible, irrational, harsh world of a church that lives as a destructive cult. (Is it any wonder that such survivors would choose to avoid *any* church, after such an experience of growing up?)

So there is a double punch of trauma in the departure from an abusive church—the expectation of rejection and shame that is inculcated while individuals are still members, and the anguish and pain members experience when they actually leave.

But healing can begin in the midst of their pain. The healing is deep, because their wounds are deep. The healing takes a long time, because their wounding took a long time. But the healing does begin—and grows with every step, every day, month, and year away from the place where they were welcomed as friends but dismissed as enemies.

Chapter 6

Let the Healing Begin!

"Is there any kind of self-care that I can do to promote healing and recovery from what I've been through?"

"Should I join a new church, or wait awhile?"

"Should I do some Bible study on the topic of abusive churches?"

"Should I pray more?"

"Should I go back and confront the abusive church? Do I even *want* to go to church?"

"Do I really feel I can trust a church, or a pastor, again?"

"What about my family—my wife and kids? How should I explain what I'm going through to them? How can I understand what *they're* going through? We're all messed up—how can we really help each other?"

"I'm going to start a detailed study of the Bible—to figure out what went wrong—how they're so wrong!"

"Bible study?! I've had my fill of that! There are plenty of other things to study!"

"Was the church really all that bad? Am I just a whiner, a malcontent, a disciple who simply didn't cut the mustard, and is now afraid to face that fact?"

These are just a few of the questions that may rattle around in the thinking of someone who has left an abusive church—many of them I asked when we left our abusive, Bible-based church in 1996. But I believe recovery from spiritual abuse—and all of its torturous subcategories of abuse, is more an issue of choosing what to *undo* than it is trying to figure out what to *do*. It's common for survivors to flee the memories of spiritual abuse by sprinting ahead without looking back.

Immediately after leaving our destructive church, Sharon and I began reengaging with an array of activities that we hoped would usher us back to the normal life we sought and help us create a healthy home for our three daughters. We were almost flat broke, having lived paycheck to paycheck for the past ten or so years. Like our narcissistic pastor, we became people who pretty much lived for the moment and rarely had any money left over by the time payday arrived. But with the help of a kindhearted property owner, who waived his policy of first and last month's rent and credit checks (we would not have passed!), we moved into a charming craftsman-style home in an old Portland neighborhood where I was born and raised.

Being back on those streets where I had played, delivered papers, and hung out with my friends was a powerful source of healing. Our house was just three blocks away from the grade-school I went to from kindergarten through 8th grade. The park I grew up playing at, the pool where I (and my father, as a boy) learned to swim were nearby. I soaked in the healing familiarity of my pre-cult life. We went right to work restoring our credit rating, getting the kids settled into their new schools, faithfully attending parent-teacher conferences, and joining a healthy church in our neighborhood. We began to reestablish the strained relationships with our families and old friends. As a veteran paramedic, I began to pursue professional advancement and was promoted to the position of field training officer. I began to take seminary classes, intent on continuing to pursue my dream of being a pastor. It was the best plan we could come up with to recover from a twelve-year ordeal. We worked hard at the program of recovery we'd created for ourselves and our daughters.

But it didn't work out very well.

We soon realized we were very, very damaged people, in a fragile marriage, with (as we later learned) severely traumatized children. We felt like a fellow survivor who described her experience in a cult—as if we had been "wounded in a war that no one knew about." Burned out from the abusive church, we were soon also burned out by our own self-composed attempts to recover from it.

So, what is a better approach to recovery from an abusive church experience?

Looking back, I'm grateful that we made it—that our marriage survived, and that our kids have all recovered pretty well from the experience, although we all still carry scars from it to this day. Even my youngest daughter, under the age of two when we left, experienced the effects of an abusive church simply by growing up in a family full of abuse survivors.

Now, years later, I see how a few practices played a powerful role in helping me recover from the abusive church. In particular, the following three practices had a profound role in my recovery from spiritual abuse. They are first steps on a pathway that I believe will lead to healing over time. I hope they will also help survivors who are reading this book.

Build Healthy, Empathetic Friendships

First, develop and enjoy friendships with like-minded souls and fellow survivors. A powerful part of healing from spiritual abuse is simply building healthy friendships with other survivors. If those survivors come from the same group—all the better. In the presence of such friends who are fellow survivors, stories can be told and retold. Thoughts, ideas, memories, and feelings can be shared and processed in an accepting, empathetic environment in which the survivors are not tempted to couch their words to avoid upsetting the sensitivities of others.

Survivors need to tell their stories of spiritual abuse. A few, sympathetic fellow survivors of an abusive church or other abusive experience can hear us say the same things, over and over, and continue to provide understanding, empathy, and affirmation, reminding us as we repeat the stories of our abuse and pain, "Yes, that is what happened." Over time, as we continue to acknowledge, name, speak about, and accept the trauma of spiritual abuse, healing continues.

Especially in the first days, weeks, and months after one leaves an abusive church, such friends are priceless. Within a few months after Sharon and I left our church, a couple dozen other members also left, and we formed a close-knit community of survivors. We met often to talk through our recovery, to remember and grieve some of the events we went through in the church, and to encourage each other in our various processes of recovery.

Along with a few fellow survivors, Sharon and I have begun a monthly meetup for survivors of spiritual abuse. The Spiritual Abuse Forum for Education (SAFE) meets in a local pub, welcomes survivors from all backgrounds and religions, and has become a great place to listen to each other share our experiences and to learn about the processes of thought-reform and spiritual abuse. Along the way, we've made some wonderful friends. Out of the eighteen or so people who attended our last meetup, I counted at least five different abusive, cult-like churches that were represented by attendees. After a couple of years of monthly meetups, we also partnered with the International Cultic Studies Association (ICSA) to host a one-day conference on spiritual abuse, attended by more than seventy people. The basis of our meetups, and even our partnership with ICSA, is to facilitate healthy friendships with like-minded souls. The education we've gained has been tremendously helpful. The friendships, priceless.

But whether it is just an informal gathering of like-minded friends, or participation in a meetup, conference, or recovery group—or all of these, there is great benefit in simply spending time with people who "get it" and won't roll their eyes or shudder when survivors tell their stories of abuse. It's a matter of seeking and creating places where survivors of spiritual abuse can feel understood and validated.

Show Yourself Some Grace

Second, grant yourself the very same grace, compassion, patience, and acceptance that you would give to others, and hope that others would give to you. We often are unkind and rejecting of ourselves, and this response hurts our recovery process. Many survivors are quite hard on themselves for years after their departure from abusive churches. They reason,

> "Nobody twisted my arm to get me into that church. I could have left it anytime I wanted, but I chose to stay."

It is true that survivors of abusive churches did decide to stay in their abuse, and now they rue doing do. But allow me to push back just a bit: If you had known when you joined the church how things would end up, the discomfort, pain, and abuse that you would encounter—would you have joined it? Of course not.

Who would join a church or group that would lead them into such turmoil and loss? No one. It is safest to assume that you were, in some manner, deceived when you were recruited into the situation. The person who recruited you may very well have been deceived, too. But you were manipulated. You weren't told the whole story of how things operated in the church, of what the leaders *really* believed, and of just how much authority over the members the leaders genuinely believed they possessed. If you had known all, or even a little, of that—you would have run for the hills, wouldn't you?

So, take it easy on yourself. Grant yourself the same benefit of doubt, and some grace. Try thinking well of yourself, without judgment and shame. Haven't you had enough of the hardened, exhausting religion of the abusive church?

Learn about Spiritual Abuse

Finally, you might benefit from some good sources to better understand the processes, lies, and control-mechanisms that have wounded you. There are great books that deal with the processes of mind control and thought reform in all areas of our culture (i.e., the military, Eastern cults, political cults, self-help groups, the sports and entertainment industries, etc.). Such groups are certainly not in and of themselves abusive—but they all have abusive leaders that victimize members within their sphere of control or responsibility.

And although Christian devotional literature can be helpful, a good balance of secular, academically based sources will greatly contribute to your understanding of what happened to you. Such authors as Lifton, Langone, Hassan, Singer, Goldberg, Enroth, and Stein, among others, have been tremendously helpful to me and my friends in our recovery from the abusive church. Also, the myriad articles available without cost on the website of the International Cultic Studies Association can provide a solid, academically oriented education on the phenomenon of cults, abusive churches, and high-demand, coercive groups.

Venturing outside of the Christian world of cultic studies and spiritual abuse has provided me with the broader vocabulary and experience that I needed to understand the whole phenomena of spiritual abuse. I have found that, in many ways, churches and seminaries have been slow to appreciate the brutal, pathological behavior of the narcissist pastor. Instead, they tend to view him as a sinful man or a troubled man or a compromised man, instead of someone with a pathological personality disorder that drives him to control, use, and traumatize those around him.

I imagine that the preceding three suggestions for recovery from spiritual values might strike you as a thin soup, and I wouldn't argue with you. You might be wondering,

"What about counseling?"

"What about finding a solid, good church?"

"What about going back to school?"

"What about beginning to rebuild the ravaged finances, the lost homes, the broken trust, the lost friendships, the ruined reputations?"

And I am not suggesting any of these areas is unimportant. In each, I wholeheartedly concur—it is imperative to rebuild a healthy life after suffering spiritual abuse. But those three things—empathetic friends, kindness to self, and exploration of solid, fact-based teaching on spiritual abuse—are three powerful resources that can start the healing process within hours of your leaving the abusive church. And they can easily exist alongside more structured, continued efforts in healing the wounds of spiritual abuse.

Those survivors who hold to the Christian faith, and desire to continue in it, will find a new challenge—can I ever again trust a church? I will directly address the issue in a later chapter, but for now, let's consider the experience of those who have left abusive churches, and then venture into a healthy church.

Chapter 7

When the Walking Wounded
Walk into Church

THE MEMBERS OF HEALTHY churches often have a tough time understanding the concept of an abusive, *Christian* church—a church that holds to correct, orthodox theology, and yet functions like a cult. Many believe that attending a church with "good doctrine" inoculates them against the cult-like, spiritually abusive conditions in their church. Moreover, statistics report that only about 2 percent of the congregation sitting in a church on a Sunday morning have experienced spiritual abuse. That's a lot of victims, but not enough to be readily recognized by the over 350,000 churches in America. As a result, very few church members today understand the experiences and trauma endured by survivors of spiritual abuse in Christian churches. And because the survivor's wounds are spiritual—invisible—they are not readily noticed. What are these wounds survivors of spiritual abuse carry with them when they walk through the doors of a healthy church?

I have asked friends who share my experience of belonging to an abusive church to describe their experiences of reentry into healthy churches. They speak of *loneliness, insecurity,* and the *prevailing fear that they are perceived as spiritually damaged goods* when they seek to worship in healthy churches. I'm not sure if we spiritual-abuse survivors really stick out as prominently as we feel like we do—but we do share that sense of unhealed woundedness we fear must be obvious to others. Many of us are compelled to find a *good, healthy* church as an issue of obedience to God, but we do so with a vague, gnawing feeling that our very reason for finding a *good* church might be a part of what led us into the abusive church in the first place. Others among us simply step back, take a break, and disengage from the whole organized worship scene, choosing against going to a church and joining its ranks again. These folks frequently do not receive much patience or understanding from their fellow Christians, who often believe that, until a survivor of an abusive church buckles down, bites the bullet, and joins another church—this time a *good* church—God won't have much to do with them.

But whether a survivor jumps right back into the church scene or steps back from it, once she *does* enter a church again, she is entering a community that believes and does many of the very same things those in the abusive church she left believed and did: Good churches sing; abusive churches sing. Good churches have powerful, persuasive preachers; abusive churches have powerful, persuasive preachers. Good churches have programs for the kids; abusive churches have programs for the kids. Good churches open the Bible for answers and direction; abusive churches open the Bible for answers and direction. Good churches collect money for their support; abusive churches collect money for their support. Good churches notice and affirm new people and visitors; abusive churches notice and affirm new people.

There are certainly many differences between a good church and an abusive church. But to a survivor of spiritual abuse, a whole lot of things look and feel the same in both churches. And now, as she comes into your church, she brings a lot of pain, hurt, and brokenness with her. She is walking, but she is wounded. With a view toward care and support, let's examine some of these wounds . . .

Wounds of the Soul

The false self. Abusive churches demand that their members create a false, church self—one that serves the demands and expectations of the church by directing the member in how to speak, act, think, decide and be compliant. The member builds a new, false self—one who does and says things that simply aren't him. He's not himself anymore, but neither is he the false self. The false self gives more money than the true self wants to give, spends more time at church than the true self wants to spend, prioritizes involvement with the church over time with family, friends, and the things he used to like to do. The false self is on duty day and night to keep him out of hot water with church leaders, and this false self applies layer after layer of inauthentic living that he soon claims as his true identity.

In fact, the member's true identity has been highjacked by the false self, and is hidden away deep in the dark, cold cellar of the member's mind. Every member of the abusive church has the two selves battling within, which forms a split personality in the member he carries with him when he leaves the church. The visible personality, expressed in church-friendly living, is the one leaders and fellow church members see. The hidden personality, the one who has been relegated to the basement and rarely is let out into public, wastes away in its forced seclusion, but it never dies. The splitting—when the member speaks and acts on the outside incongruently with what he believes and desires on the inside—does horrible damage to his mental health. Such cognitive dissociation makes him a type of walking civil war from an emotional-psychiatric perspective.

But what of the *core self*, the true, God-given personality each human being is born with—our souls? I believe that our souls are a creation of God, and God never relinquishes ownership of his creation. We can ruin our souls, neglect them, starve them, ignore them, damage them beyond all recognition—but in the end, they belong to God, and in some way, never stop being a small reflection of his image.

And as I reflect on my experience of being spiritually abused, I believe my soul, the inner *me*, was always working to get me out of my abusive, cultic church. It nagged me, itched my conscience, gnawed at my thoughts, and, in the end, like a whack-a-mole game, simply kept popping up. Finally, it won out, and I shed the fake me like a snake shedding its skin. But the process was long and excruciating.

So under such a weight of mental stress, what are some of the wounds of the soul that members in the spiritually abusive church suffer and carry with them when they leave? Survivors experience *flashbacks* when numerous later circumstances, interactions, and conditions that correspond to conditions and experiences in the abusive church remind them of their experience there. Such episodes may trigger responses that may seem inappropriate or extreme. An authoritative, charismatic, talented preacher, for instance, can trigger survivors into feeling the same emotions and tensions they experienced under the preaching of the abusive pastor, if that pastor was such a preacher. A casual statement from the new pastor affirming the positive, beneficial results of regular attendance, financial support, or even the practice of a healthy spiritual discipline, can trigger survivors into experiencing the same emotions they did when those personal, spiritual disciplines were demanded of them in the abusive church. The simple phrase *the Bible says* can cause survivors to brace themselves for the blow to come—as they mistakenly anticipate the Bible will be used to demand, control, and strip away their autonomy.

Depression. Survivors struggle with *depression*, including persistent feelings of sadness, anxiety, purposelessness, pessimism, joylessness, and exhaustion. The level of depression the survivors of spiritual abuse experience often merits medical and psychiatric intervention in the form of counseling, antidepressant medication, and even physical therapies designed to help them in their recovery. One of the most harmful results of pastors not appreciating the phenomena of abusive churches and Christian cults is that they are slow to refer survivors to the specialized counseling and medical care that can provide significant assistance in their recovery from spiritual abuse.

Self-medication. Survivors struggle with *self-medicating* as they seek to alleviate emotional pain and stress through a variety of substances and activities. They might abuse drugs, whether prescribed by a doctor or scored on the street. Alcohol can provide the nightly relaxation they require to be able to sleep or to take the edge off their fear of going to work or church. They might also use sex to distract themselves from emotional pain, or resort to unhealthy overeating. They might begin to work out way too much and too hard. I often ask those who have recently exited a high-demand group, abusive church, or cult if they are self-medicating with alcohol, drugs, or other harmful behaviors, and if they acknowledge that they are, suggest they would benefit from a visit to a primary-care physician. They may have begun self-medicating when they were in the abusive church, and that may have been tolerated, encouraged, and even exemplified by its leaders. Abusive churches do not produce or sustain healthy people.

Guilt. Survivors often struggle with *guilt.* They may have compromised personal standards of ethical speech or behavior. They feel guilty for the things they said and did while they were in the church. They are sure that, somehow, somewhere deep down, they must shoulder some blame for their abuse. It's a hard sell to get a religiously inclined person who has left what was a very straight-jacketed, legalistic church to embrace the grace of God. Deep down, survivors of spiritual abuse long for the very blessings and assurances of the gospel that they (usually) already believe and even may have knocked on doors to tell their neighbors about.

Shame. Survivors struggle with *shame.* Shame, while closely tied to guilt, is much worse. It is toxic to the soul of its carrier. Shame is the result of mixing up what we do with who we are. We feel guilt over the wrong things we do; we feel shame for who we believe we are. We do something wrong, bad, hurtful, and then we feel guilty, as we should. But when we do or say something wrong, deceitful, dishonest, and then surmise that we therefore are unworthy people—that is shame. We feel we are unworthy of respect . . . courtesy . . . kindness . . . forgiveness . . . deserving of being hurt and abused by our pastor. . . . Things like that. Shame suffocates our souls—pounding into them the message that we don't deserve the air we breathe.

Abusive leaders of abusive churches may have shamed members through public (group) condemnation; mock trials (often with a twisted, *ecclesial* tone to them); or private, one-on-one *discipleship* meetings with a spiritual mentor. Sadly, although the members may successfully walk away from their abusive churches, they often carry destructive feelings of shame for many years after they have left.

Anger and blame. Survivors of spiritual abuse are often *angry*. They are offended and provoked as they come to grips with what the leader and the group did to them. As time passes, they may better understand the unstable, vulnerable position they were in when they were recruited into the church, and how the leaders took advantage of their condition. Improperly processed, this anger can be misdirected, resulting in all sorts of self-loathing and nastiness toward others, and even God.

When I left the church, I was enraged at God within weeks, blaming him for the twelve years there that I accounted for as wasted and devastating to my family. "So, is *that* the way you answer the prayers of twenty-two-year-olds who want to serve you?! *That's* what you do when they ask you to lead them . . . send them to a *cult*?! You are one lousy Father, God," I railed. "Thanks a lot!"

However, the anger can also be something positive. While misdirecting our anger can delay recovery from spiritual abuse, we should not fear it, for something terrible *has* happened. As abuse survivors, we *were* mistreated, disrespected, and used. *Of course,* we are angry!

Ambiguity. Survivors struggle to accept the *ambiguity* of many theological, faith-related issues because they believe their views on those issues are unambiguously, irrefutably correct and purely logical. Abusive churches and cults do not teach their members to tolerate diversity of opinion. Instead, they insist that there is one way, their way, and that all other views are simply wrong. There is no room for *either/or* in the belief and assumptions of the abusive church in such areas as politics; social issues; gender roles in the church and home, including the relationship of husbands and wives; the education of children; styles of music; social standards; dietary practices; or a citizen's obligations to the government. For members who leave such totalist ideology and teaching, it is very difficult and confusing to accept that other Christians simply disagree about some issues that were held by the abusive church as litmus tests for the authenticity of faith, and often, salvation itself. And it can be particularly challenging for those who have left such monolithic, *our-way-or-the-highway* thinking to navigate the waters of today's mixed-up, wildly pluralistic world.

Conflicting emotions. The mix of feelings and attitudes listed previously can make things pretty messy in a survivor's head. After leaving my abusive church, I experienced a bizarre combination of self-loathing and self-righteousness, especially during the worship services of the *normal* churches I attended. I recall sitting in a Sunday service just months after I had left, inwardly criticizing the music, the content of the sermon, and the skills of the preacher. As I thumbed through the worship guide, I judged what seemed to me the church's shallow programs and lack of biblical vision and focus.

But only moments later, I was overcome with excruciating shame, self-condemnation, and insecurity. I whispered to Sharon,

"I have got to go. See you at home."

Five minutes later, there I was, head down, shuffling down the street, with one step hating the church, with the next hating myself. It can be tough for the survivors of abusive churches to simply show up to worship, give themselves a break, and remain for the whole service.

Sleep issues. Survivors experience *sleep disorders* and *nightmares.* I still have dreams, most of which do not rate as out-and-out *nightmares.* I think my dreams are a type of self-healing, as my subconscious is attempting to heal my conscious memories. Patterns of *being back there* are common, with me reliving the horrible stress of the abusive church, but often openly questioning or criticizing its leaders. I think those dreams are an attempt to allow me to relive the experiences, only this time (in the dream) working on making things turn out better than they did in real life. When new conditions arise that are related to the old church (court trials, news accounts, running into members in public, etc.) I often have a few nights of the old "cult dreams," as my wife and I have come to call them.

There are plenty more variations on the wounds I have summarized here. Survivors of abusive churches and pastors struggle with overwhelming, gnawing feelings of isolation, loneliness, insecurity, lack of confidence, embarrassment, indecisiveness, and a host of other emotional maladies. Generally, if persons experience a sense of woundedness *after* the spiritual abuse that they did not experience *before* the abuse—it makes sense that their wounds are the result of that spiritual abuse.

Wounds of Faith

Survivors of spiritual abuse carry significant spiritual wounds. They may have substantial disappointments and unresolved struggles in their views on religion, God, the church, Christians in general, and Christianity as a valid belief system. They are likely to have unanswered questions regarding the Bible, the church, and anything that touches on the religious motives and passions that drew them to the church in the first place. It is likely they joined the church without a great deal of input from outsiders. While they were members of the church, it is unlikely they engaged in much critical thinking, or in prayer or meditation that dared to veer away from the unique beliefs of their church.

Survivors often harbor deep disappointment with God. Some question the existence of God. Others, believing in God's existence, question the idea that he has their best interests in mind, or even notices them at all. Were they wrong to think God would really lead them and care for them? And what about the Christian beliefs they were indoctrinated to adhere to so strongly, and to which they submitted every big decision in life? Some of the great theological themes in the Bible, such as the sovereignty of God, his providence, leadership, protection, and love for people, are difficult for survivors to believe as they struggle to heal from wounds they received in the house of God. Many survivors of spiritual abuse have, in a sense, broken up with God, or have settled into a don't-call-me-I'll-call-you kind of relationship him.

It is critical that survivors of abusive churches be shown gracious acceptance should they choose to stop attending church services, refuse to become a member of a church, or stop identifying as Christian. (If the last point seems excessive, inappropriate, or simply unfaithful, then you may not be grasping the depth of pain and loss that those who have been abused in the church have experienced.) As far as they're concerned, they've done their time living on the edge for the Lord—they've counted the cost, paid it, run up their credit for it, and sold their grandma's wedding ring to a pawnshop for it. Now, they are (often) as emptied of spiritual reserves as they are of material, and they simply need a break, no matter how healthy the church you hope they will visit.

Marriage Wounds

Marriages do not do very well in the abusive church, for narcissistic pastors are offended and suspicious of the exclusive loyalty marriage entails between spouses. Often, such pastors bear a general suspicion and animosity toward all dyadic (two-person) relationships in their church. Any exclusive, unique relationship between two people (husband-wife, parent-child, friend-friend, etc.) constitutes a threat, and is therefore discouraged, ignored, or invaded. They are jealous of any and every two-person relationship in which they are not one of the two persons! In speaking of this phenomenon in cult leaders, therapist Lorna Goldberg has written, "Cult leaders need to be the most important figure in the life of each member. To achieve this, cult leaders need to control every significant aspect of a member's life."[1] And it is in the relationships between spouses and between parents and children that abusive pastors and cult leaders do some of their most horrible damage.

Abusive pastors may infuse suspicion and division into the marriage relationships of their followers, demanding that no secrets between spouses are kept from the leader. Spouses are pressured

1. Goldberg, "Reflections on Marriage and Children."

to divulge their respective mate's personal issues, failures, and even statements made in the privacy of the home. In its extreme forms, this interference with the marriage relationship may even include abusive leaders prying into the intimate, sexual areas of the marriage under the guise of *counseling, encouragement,* or *discipleship,* but with the actual intent of unraveling the intimate safety marriage partners share. In the abusive church, any loyalty that is not centered on the leader(s) of the church is attacked, destroyed, or redirected back to the leaders. As an example, the simple demand for attendance at the many services and programs and meetings of the church, along with private meetings with leaders and teachers, can drain members of the time needed to relax and enjoy time with a spouse. Survivors who have experienced such abuse of their marriages often struggle with trusting their spouses, and they wonder whether their marriage can be saved, or if it is worth saving.

For those marriages that began in the abusive church, achieving a healthy marriage is especially difficult because the only identity that either spouse knows of his or her mate within the marriage is that of the fellow member of the abusive church, and not the *pre-church* individual. But whether their marriage began before the couple's membership in the abusive church or after they joined, the church's attack on the marriage is ruthless, deep, and lasting. Is it any surprise that they would hesitate to step into a church again after having their marriage attacked and slighted in a church? Can anyone blame them for deciding to step back from church attendance and instead take a deep breath on Sunday mornings, relaxing together over a quiet breakfast before going on a hike or to a movie?

Parenting Wounds

The wounds of regret and guilt can be overwhelming for parents who have subjected their children to a church that hurt them. Having believed they were raising their children in the most positive, spiritually healthy way, they have had to face that they led their children into a church experience in which their dear children received deep, lasting wounds.

For Sharon and me, the church we believed would provide the best life, spiritual education, and positive experience of our Christian faith ended up robbing our children of joy and faith itself. For a while, it also shook their ability to trust Sharon and me.

On a winter evening in 1996. Sharon and I and our three daughters were at the dinner table, talking about the start of school for the older girls, Bryn, then twelve, and Rachel, then ten. (Our youngest, Grace, was almost two.) The subject of the abusive church we had left months earlier came up often at mealtime. (Did I just write "often"? It's really about all we ever talked about.)

"Do you think we'll ever go back there?" asked Bryn.

"Yeah," her ten-year-old sister quietly asked, "are we going back?"

Sharon and I looked at each other with a look that said, *Go slow and easy on this one—they lost all their friends when we left the church.* Our kids were all born while we were members of the church, and Bryn and Rachel had spent all their young lives in it, living semi-communally for six of the years we were members. The other children in the church were like siblings to them. They spent countless hours with the same kids, learning to walk at the same time, having little-girl tea parties together, loving the same toys, playing on the same Little League teams, worshipping the same pop stars, and attending the same schools. We knew that when we'd left the abusive church we'd also suddenly, forcibly separated the girls from their best friends.

And with each day of freedom from the church, our certainty that we would certainly never return only grew. The girls had already begun the school year in their new schools and were enjoying exploring their new neighborhood. Going back to the church was out of the question, its spell over us long broken. Now, we were faced with what we believed to be a critical challenge—telling our daughters we would never return to the church, and to their dearest friends.

73

"Well," I began, "we're not so sure about it . . ."

Sharon continued, "Because we're not sure it's where we really want to be, as far as . . ."

". . . what's best for our family," I finished.

The table was silent as the girls looked from Sharon's face to mine, trying to figure out what might come out of our mouths next.

"So, no; we're not going to go back. Ever?"

"No, we're never going back. Ever."

There, I thought. *We said it.* After a brief, awkward pause, both Brynny and Rachel looked at each other, and then got up from the table. I looked at Sharon, whose face revealed the same worry that I was feeling. *Oh, no*, I thought. *They are going to run to their rooms. They're crushed, disappointed. It's going to be a long night. Dad disappoints, yet again.*

But they did not run to their rooms. Instead, they giggled, locked arms, and began swirling around the kitchen floor like exuberant square dancers, chanting,

"We're never going back! We're *never* going back! We're *never* going back!"

Sharon and I stared, open-mouthed, both thinking, *What have we done to these kids?* There we sat at the kitchen table in stunned silence, watching the spontaneous, joy-filled dance of freedom on our kitchen floor, and realizing in yet another way how we had really gotten it all so wrong. (In the near future, we would learn what had happened to several of the girls in the abusive church, and the unrestrained joy of our daughters that evening would make more sense to us.)

Parents who expose their children to spiritually abusive churches face great hurdles in the recovery process after the family has left. They may carry crushing guilt for using methods of discipline on their kids that were harsh, painful, and simply abusive. They may reflect on their parenting experiences and see that they were uninvolved and neglectful, quick to dish out punishment and correction, slow to shower grace and unconditional love.

Parents may grieve the degree to which they granted other, non-related adults the authority to correct and discipline their children, and to act as parental figures. (Spiritual abusers are infamous for their insistence on being treated as parental figures by the children in their churches.) They may face the painful realization that their children viewed the abusive pastor with the same fear, loyalty, and submissiveness as their parents had viewed him. They may worry that their children seem slow to abandon their loyalty and affection for the abusive pastor.

The parents grieve over the lost resources of money, time, and energy that went to the abusive church and not to their children. As their children begin to believe they truly are free of the abusive church, they may begin to relate their experiences to their parents of what life was like for them in the cult, including examples of emotional, physical, and in some cases, sexual abuse. The parents' confidence withers as they realize how extensive the effect of the spiritually abusive church was on their children, who memorized verse after verse of the Bible while also memorizing whom to obey, whom to fear, and how to survive and avoid trauma in the abusive church.

There is perhaps no greater responsibility in life than that of parenting a child. It is a bitter thing to grasp the fact that your kids, who had no choice in the matter, were abused in the church that Mom and Dad raised them in. As I discuss in coming pages, this is a burden that loving, understanding, empathetic friends, pastors, and extended family members can help to bear in caring for parents who survive abusive churches.

Economic Wounds

Abusive churches do not exist to make people happy, satisfied, and spiritually healthy. Rather, they exist to take all kinds of things from their members, and perhaps more than anything, their members' money. The survivors of abusive churches often are struggling financially, and fighting, scrimping, and saving to regain financial stability. Some are at a stage of life when they expected they would own homes, be secure in their professions, and have retirement savings; but they often have none of those resources and are starting over to build wealth. Even now, it still pains me to think of the lost income, both real and potential, of those twelve years we were under the domination of an abusive pastor. I suppose everyone makes bad financial decisions in life and ends up with fewer dollars in the bank as a result. But the feeling of being ripped off, deceived, and squeezed in the name of Jesus stings, and it takes a while to get over that.

Educational and Professional Wounds

Many survivors have neglected to pursue educational and professional goals. They will feel they have lost opportunities for advancement in the workplace and have left their dreams and goals on the altar of loyalty to the abusive churches and pastors. Some may have put career plans on hold, having been told by their abusive leaders that they instead should be investing their time and energies in the abusive church. They may have been told that, as the church grew, there would be opportunities for paid service, perhaps even as pastors themselves, if they would only hold on and keep on giving to the church. And they gave and gave—and left with nothing.

Survivors of spiritually abusive churches often walk through the doors of healthy churches feeling like professional and academic failures. They feel like unfortunate, spiritual gamblers who have cast the dice in a bid for greater meaning and productivity as Christians and thrown snake eyes.

These are just some of the main areas of trauma and woundedness that the survivors of spiritual abuse bear as they recover. They don't leave these wounds at home on Sunday when they seek a healthy church in which to worship, and they don't leave them in the car in the parking lot either. The wounds of spiritual abuse come right through the door with the survivors and are, in fact, the wounds they hope to find care for in the healthy church.

Chapter 8

The Pastor as a Safe Shepherd

PASTOR RALPH DIDN'T KNOW much of what had happened to us in the abusive church we had left just a few months earlier. Sharon and I felt very strongly that, for the sake of our daughters, we should find a good church to go to, even though neither of us felt much of a desire to attend. We wanted for them to make friends in a good church, and to participate in its programs and ministries to kids. When we visited a small neighborhood church near our home, we were immediately impressed by its friendliness, safe environment, relaxed worship and teaching, and the kindness and humility of the pastor, Ralph.

Pastor Ralph remembered our names and our kids' names. He was friendly and kind, but never intrusive or pushy. For the first couple of months we attended (with somewhat spotty regularity), our main contact with Ralph was on Wednesday nights, when he would hang out in the foyer talking with the kids after their youth meetings, high-fiving, shaking hands, and giving a hearty good-bye as the kids got into their parents' cars. He also would wave at the parents, sometimes greeting them by name.

We watched him closely. *Very* closely.

Survivors of high-demand groups are often anxious when they go to church. They observe the behavior of the church members, and especially the pastors, before venturing to open up about their own personal experiences of spiritual abuse. They need to be able to choose anonymity as they take time to trust churches and church leaders. Healthy church members and their pastors understand this need.

After a few months at the new church, we asked to meet with Pastor Ralph. We were in crisis because our daughters had shared something with us from their experience in the abusive church that had shaken us, and we needed some help. Sharon and I went to the home of Pastor Ralph and his wife, Lois, for coffee and dessert one evening. We hemmed and hawed about the church we had left, about its abusive pastor, its heavy-handed control of members, its strange communal living arrangements, and how we had been mistreated and misled. I doubt we really divulged anything that made us look too strange or made our former church look too horrible (although we sure could have!). Nevertheless, as we shared our experience with Pastor Ralph, I sensed he knew there was more to our story than we had shared. We told him of the abuse, the rules, the demand for money, time, and obedience that our pastor had inflicted on us.

"Well, that's crazy! I can't believe that a pastor could act like that! And he went to seminary?" Ralph asked, referring to our former pastor. "A legitimate seminary?"

"Well . . . he took a few classes, and then he dropped out. He only wanted to study Greek, Hebrew, and theology and did not want to take what he called the 'marrying and burying' classes," we told him.

"He should have taken the other classes . . . might have learned a few things," Ralph wryly commented.

There was an awkward pause.

Sharon spoke. "But we just found out he . . . the girls. . . . Our daughters told us . . . he . . ."

I looked into Ralph's face, and saw his jaw clench.

". . . that they were . . . molested. By the pastor. He molested them."

At that instant Ralph's leg violently extended forward, his foot slamming into the coffee table in front of him, sending cups, saucers, forks, and plates rattling across its surface. His spine snapped straight, throwing him against the backrest of the couch.

Startled, we pulled back. I expected Ralph to swear, but he didn't—out loud, anyway. His face showed a depth of anger and intensity that I had never seen before from this kindhearted, friendly pastor. In an instant, his rage set us all back and made the room feel electrically charged. It also made us feel loved.

Pastor Ralph was not an expert on abusive churches and had not studied thought reform and cults. But he *was* a genuine, loving, experienced pastor. He had spent many years in ministry, had seen a lot, and had made hard choices of sacrifice, obscurity, and integrity. His battle-toughened exterior covered a sensitive, good heart; and when he heard of the sexual abuse of two of the children who attended his church, sexual abuse by a spiritual fraud who dared call himself a pastor, Ralph could not contain his fury. I think he would have attacked our former pastor, had he been in the room, in the same way a shepherd would attack any predator that threatened his beloved flock. I think, at that moment, Ralph would have broken the molesting pastor's jaw. In seminary, I was taught the skills and information that a good pastor needs to have in his head. In Pastor Ralph's living room, I saw the passion and love that a faithful pastor must have in his heart.

Lois had immediately looked in on us from the kitchen to ask what the ruckus was in the living room. We said,

"Oh, nothing. Everything's fine."

But I could have said, "Pastor Ralph is showing us what it looks like to be a great pastor."

Over the years I've come to believe that Christians need great pastors more than they need great preachers. There are many opportunities to hear great preaching today—both past and present—not only in church on Sunday, but also on the radio and the Internet. A person can go through the day listening to one sermon after another, preached by men and women with powerful, riveting, rhetorical skill. But people who have been abused and mistreated in what they believed to be the house of God need something other than great preaching. They need the tenderhearted love and care of great pastors, men and women who have bowed to their knees before the Great Pastor, and who refuse to act or speak in any way that does not follow his example of sacrificial, loving care for people.

Most pastors feel they are ill equipped to respond to the needs of the survivors of abusive churches. Aside from the broad discussion of those religious groups historically deemed *cults* by orthodox, evangelical Christianity, seminaries do not provide extensive training in how to address the phenomenon of churches that abuse their members with a cultish fanaticism and arrogance. But just as the proper care of a physical wound is necessary for successful healing and recovery, a proper response to the wounds the survivors of spiritual abuse have experienced is indispensable.

In their efforts to care for survivors of spiritual abuse, pastors and church leaders may be tempted to resort to an academic approach, acting as information sources through an array of small-group studies, formal Bible studies, and doctrinally sound preaching. But the survivors of an abusive church have most likely had their fill of doctrinally sound, orthodox teaching and preaching. Whether or not their spiritually abusive church was Bible-based, they may have difficulty finding healing through Bible study. They have likely spent a significant amount of time in their abusive church studying the Bible. They may be familiar with the works of contemporary and historic theologians. They may have a strong ability to study the Bible on their own. But more Bible study is rarely the answer for someone who has perhaps spent years studying the Bible in an abusive—and often so-called—Bible church!

Pastors may also feel that participation in a small group that focuses on building solid friendships with church members is what survivors need: that if they can just get *locked in* to a close, small group that is healthy and begin to make some friends, then healing will begin. Again, such a plan for recovery can be problematic because survivors have likely left a group in which they had close friendships, developed over years and intensified by the shared experience of zeal and commitment to their church. The experience of attending a (new) small-group meeting before a survivor is ready can be traumatic and unpleasant, even with the best-intentioned small group.

Some pastors believe that simply attending a healthy church will bring healing to the survivor of spiritual abuse, as if a person with an infection could be cured simply by spending time around people who do not have infections! They assume that simply hearing historically orthodox preaching will heal the survivor of the wounds of spiritual abuse; but often, the survivor has sat under powerful, doctrinally sound preaching for years within the abusive environment. And sitting under the preaching of an authoritative, rhetorically powerful, charismatic speaker who preaches from the Bible will do little in itself to heal the wounds inflicted by an abusive, authoritative, rhetorically powerful, charismatic speaker who preaches from the Bible!

If our small groups, Bible studies, church activities, and biblical preaching are not likely to bring the healing of spiritual abuse, what will? For instance, what can a pastor offer to a person who ventures into a worship service on a Sunday morning and reveals that tiny tip of an iceberg that suggests the person has been hurt by an abusive, high-demand church? I believe it all has to do with the initial tone and friendliness with which the pastor treats the individual. A gracious welcome lasting no more than a few minutes or even seconds, before or after a worship service, can begin to suggest to the survivor the possibility of healing and restoration. However, it's important for the pastor to consider the following insights.

- The first thing to realize is that the survivors of abusive churches have chosen to visit this church because of its similarities to the beliefs of the abusive church they left. I know that sounds pretty strange, so let me explain: People who leave abusive churches have not abandoned all of their values and beliefs about their religious faith. Studies have demonstrated that people who leave abusive, high-control groups

82

do not abandon all of the beliefs held by their former groups.[1] As a pastor, I am a bit humbled when I realize that at least a part of the reason the survivors of spiritual abuse visit my church is because my church shares some of the beliefs of their abusive church!

- Those who seek a new, healthy church after leaving an abusive Christian church need to be treated as wounded brothers and sisters in the faith. They should not be evangelized or proselytized when they visit the church. If they are unclear or undecided regarding the basic truths of the gospel, there will be time for that later, when they continue to attend the church and suitable, healthy relationships develop with the pastor and church members.

  Survivors develop a *sixth sense* that identifies hidden motives and unspoken intentions. They're mind readers; so, a pastor dealing with abuse survivors must always be extra candid, sensitive, patient, and honest. If the pastor's words are veiled set-ups for a gospel presentation, the survivors will see that coming a mile away. Better to just come out with it if necessary: "So, with all you've been through, how are things with you and God—if you don't mind me asking?"

- Pastors need a basic understanding of thought reform and how it works in abusive churches. Gaining such an understanding is often a tremendous, empowering experience for survivors of spiritual abuse. Simply by pointing survivors to some good educational resources, pastors communicate that they understand the issue, believe the survivors, and respect their ability to take personal steps of recovery. Many survivors of abusive churches are asking themselves, *What just happened to me!?* A pastor who has done a bit of preparation will be able to give them an answer and a direction to go to pursue more information.

- Pastors must avoid trying to recruit survivors of spiritual abuse to church membership. The survivors have likely

1. Jacobs, "Deconversion from Religious Movements," 294.

escaped a church that had an overweening desire for numerical growth, coupled with a need to extract membership commitments, covenants, and promises of loyalty to the church. It is simply enough to say, "Thank you so much for being here today; you're always welcome here."

In the church I serve, survivors of spiritual abuse often tell me of their experience only *after* the worship service. I think they want to evaluate the *feel* of the church and gain an impression of me before they *out* themselves as having belonged to an abusive church. That makes perfect sense to me. You might ask, "Okay, Ken, but what about people who only *claim* to have come from an abusive church, but who are actually just disgruntled ex-members of a good church?"

Every pastor has the experience of unhappy, dissatisfied people leaving their church over their disagreement or dissatisfaction with the church, only to visit a new church and promptly complain of the "horrible pastor" of their old church! I have found, however, that when pastors and church leaders gain a firm grasp on the common elements of spiritual abuse, they will readily get a feel for the genuineness of people's stories. It is likely that, as the survivors open up small parts of their stories of spiritual abuse, they will recount many of the very signs of abusive churches and victim woundedness that I have presented in this book.

- Pastors should develop a list of qualified, trusted, mental health professionals to whom they can refer survivors. Not all require care from a mental health professional, but on their path of recovery from spiritual abuse, many do. Meaningful discussions and friendships with other spiritual abuse survivors, along with education, have proven to be of great assistance in recovery. However, many survivors will benefit greatly from the wise, professional assistance of a counselor who is well informed regarding the processes of thought reform and coercion that occur in abusive churches. I suggest that a pastor *not* refer a survivor of spiritual abuse to a counselor whose method of assistance is to uncover the supposed sin in the survivor's experience of which he or she must confess in order to find healing and relief. Such an approach diminishes the damage that abusive pastors inflict and dismisses the real trauma of the client.

- In relating to survivors of spiritual abuse, the pastor must be humble and gentle. Victims of abuse have been deceived and hurt by pastoral imposters—ecclesial predators who donned the appearance of legitimacy, all the while seeking to use, steal, and ravage the members. For the most part, pastors are well educated, confident, and have developed the ability to speak with great power and persuasiveness. They can be very intimidating without even realizing it, and they must always bear in mind the survivors' need for a gentle, encouraging voice from the pastor.

  Pastors must be, primarily, who they have been called to be—shepherds. No church that abuses members is led by a genuine, Christian shepherd, and that is what its pastor must aspire to be. Pastors who are interested, emotionally connected, and unhurried will make an impression on abuse survivors who visit their churches.

Pastoring is tough work if it is done correctly and honestly. Besides living with the same ups and downs, the great days and dark days that everyone encounters, the pastor also bears the emotional weight of caring for the members of his church. It can be wearing to hear the stories survivors of spiritual abuse tell, and to commit to walking with them through their recovery from that abuse. Pastors learn things from survivors about other pastors, some of whom they may even know, or perhaps with whose ministries they have been impressed. Pastors are often disappointed to realize they are not trusted by a survivor and are judged on the basis of how much or how little they are like the pastor who abused the member. Pastors who are helping survivors are often unsure of what exactly they should do, or say, or recommend for healing.

But they are not without resources. They have experience using the Bible to help people heal, not to control or abuse them.

They have the inner sense of calling to the ministry by God, and the confidence that he will certainly empower and equip them for any challenge he sends. And they have the further assurance that they do not stand alone in their efforts to help those who have been spiritually abused. They stand with the other members of their church.

Chapter 9

The Safe Church

THERE IS NO NEED for pastors and church members to become experts on cults and abusive churches in order to help the survivors of spiritual abuse. What is required is simply that a church and its pastor aspire to conduct themselves according to what the Bible teaches regarding how all people are to be treated and valued.

He has told you, O man, what is good; And what does the LORD require of you But to do justice, to love kindness, And to walk humbly with your God? (Mic 6:8). Those who claim to be people of faith are to be fair and honest and to treat people with kindness as they live out their faith lives before God.

Let all bitterness and wrath and anger and clamor and slander be put away from you, along with all malice. Be kind to one another, tender-hearted, forgiving each other, just as God in Christ also has forgiven you (Eph 4:31–32). The church is to be a place where people do not hassle each other, fight with each other, hate each other, or live in states of animosity and disrespect for each other. Instead, it is to be a community of kind, tenderhearted people who love and forgive, as they themselves have been loved and forgiven by God. And just as the antithesis of the abusive pastor is the humble, loving pastor, the antithesis of the abusive church is the gracious, accepting church.

Churches have an amazing power—often, tragically unrealized—to be the healing agents that God calls his people to be in this beloved, hurting world. The promise of spiritual empowerment, along with the biblical testimony of God's tremendous concern and compassion for victims of spiritual abuse,[1] should give church members great confidence that, when God brings survivors of spiritual abuse to your church, that is invitation enough to care, and to be available to help them in their recovery. They could have gone to other churches, but they came to your church. With that in mind, here are a few marks of a healthy, safe church for survivors of spiritual abuse.

Safe Churches Are Honest

Whereas abusive churches recruit and retain their members through deception, and what they promise to members is never given, healthy churches do not attract members by promising experiences, benefits, and results that they have no desire or ability to provide. Their members demonstrate honesty and transparency in day-to-day life throughout the week. In all aspects, from the pulpit to the pew, and in the most informal, mundane interactions, truth is valued and practiced at all times. And besides simply telling the truth, safe churches refuse to make promises that they cannot keep, or to suggest that God is going to do things he hasn't clearly promised to do. They do not freely invite people into the life of the church, only to later make demands the members must keep in order to remain in good standing. They do not bait and switch, and the kindness and warmth with which members are received on their first visit is extended to them on every visit, whether they formally join the church or not.

Safe Churches Do Not Pressure Members to Give

In the abusive church, members are prized for the material and immaterial resources that are extracted from them. They are groomed to feel guilty if they do not give until it hurts. Safe

1. For example, Ezek 34:15–16.

churches, however, seek to give *to* their members. The financial state of the church is shared with openness and honesty, but never in a way that manipulates or frightens members. Safe churches do not throw out percentages of expected giving, such as those that demand a *tithe* (10 percent) of their members' income. They freely acknowledge that the church depends on the voluntary contributions of members, but they never employ manipulation, guilt-tripping, or worry-mongering regarding the church's financial circumstances. The leaders of safe churches are sensitive to the specific life circumstances of their members, and respectful of the great financial burdens that many members are facing.

Safe churches have distinct, relaxed attitudes toward money, born out of a confidence that they are providing an important service, and that truly they are merely extending the generosity of God—whom they expect to meet their needs as they continue to do their best to care for people. They are respectful of the privacy of their members, never prying into their personal finances or resources. The leaders exemplify trust in God for the church's financial needs by fully respecting the freedom of church members to give according to their desire and conscience, and not by compulsion or guilt (2 Cor 9:7). The pastor maintains a purposeful ignorance of the giving amounts and patterns of individual members, to avoid any suggestion that might taint the reputation of the church and the pastor. Safe churches focus on the positive, good things they desire to give *to* their members, rather than on the resources they desire their members to give over to the church.

Safe churches are also respectful of the time and energy of their members. They do not demand attendance at a growing array of church-focused meetings designed to serve the pastor and the church. They are sensitive to the many challenges of raising children in today's world, especially with the likely necessity that both parents work to meet the family's needs. In safe churches, young families are protected, and parents are encouraged to put their family's needs first, and not sacrifice time with children and spouses through taking on too many church and ministry responsibilities.

Safe Churches Encourage Healthy Friendships with Non-Christians

Whereas the elitism and ingrown relational tendencies of abusive churches prevent their members from forming or maintaining close friendships with non-Christians, safe churches never criticize or usurp the relationships its members have with those who do not share the Christian faith. Rather than seeking the dissolution of members' relationships with family and friends, whether Christian or not, a healthy church encourages satisfying, healthy relationships between all people. The biblical commands to "honor all people" and "show every consideration for all men" are followed in healthy churches, without distinction or reservation.[2] Safe churches encourage their members to treat all people for who they are: beloved people whom the God of all creation saw as worthy of sending his Son to save and redeem.

Safe Churches Respect Other Churches

Abusive churches routinely poison their members' perceptions of neighboring churches and pastors, suggesting that they are substandard, uncommitted to the Christian faith, and even worthy of disdain or pity. Safe churches, however, welcome friendship with other churches. They are generous and tolerant of differences between themselves and other churches, and seek to relate to the churches and their members as spiritual family members, not as competitors or opponents in ministry. They are secure in their own faith, and in the beliefs of the church, and see no need to attack other churches that might differ on minor or secondary issues of faith. They simply do not speak the language of exclusivity and elitism.

2. Titus 3:2; 1 Pet 2:17.

Safe Churches Encourage Self-Confidence and Independent Thinking

Abusive churches insist on occupying an expansive, expanding place in the lives of their members. They seek the growing dependence of the members on the church. Safe churches foster the growth of mature, healthy independence. They discourage overdependence on leaders or the church body itself, and instead commend members' independent, positive, personal development as followers of Jesus Christ. They do not exist to create followers who obey orders in a hierarchal structure, but instead friends of Jesus who voluntarily join the church to share in a life of worship, friendship, and service.

Safe Churches Handle Confession Appropriately

In abusive churches, compulsory confession serves the leadership, erodes the health of the community, and hurts the persons who confess. Safe churches, however, respect the privacy and dignity of their members, and never compel them to confess private sins in a public or group setting. Generally, sins are to be confessed in private, and in cases of criminal activity, police and appropriate authorities must be involved.

The sins that members most often need to confess to one another are those of mistreatment, disrespect, and insensitivity. Jesus taught that the first step of the process of forgiveness takes place in private discourse,[3] and that when we ignore offenses, our religious observances become meaningless.[4]

Safe churches are careful to admonish their members to practice a regular, mostly personal, spiritual discipline of the confession of sin.[5] They disdain the abuse of confession, and they seek to be places of forgiveness, reconciliation, and hope, rather than interrogation and emotional torture.

3. Matt 18:15.
4. Matt 5:23–24.
5. 1 John 1:9.

Safe Churches Are Kind and Respectful to Members Who Leave

A consistent quality of abusive churches is that they make the very idea of leaving, of simply moving on to a new, different church, the equivalent of abandoning one's faith. Safe churches simply never send their departing members on their way with criticism and rejection. The leaders of safe churches understand that, especially in our present culture, people not only change their jobs and careers many times throughout their working years, but they also often move to do so. It would never occur to the members of a healthy church that they should demand that fellow members determine such issues as where they live, whom they marry, what schools their children attend, and what jobs they have (and what job opportunities they decline) according to the requirement that they never leave their church.

Also, a healthy, safe church is non-controlling and respectful regarding how it says farewell to those members and frequent guests who decide to leave or simply decide not to return. A safe church holds its members loosely and gently and says goodbye with kindness and warmth. The pastors and leaders of the safe church communicate with those who leave, for they are eager to be assured that the member has not been offended, hurt, or mistreated. The safe church is concerned that all members know they are valued, respected, and always welcome to return to the church. I fear that we sometimes make it difficult for people to join our churches by communicating how difficult it will be to leave!

Safe Churches Are Saturated with Grace

Grace is the unbridled, undeserved, nearly incomprehensible kindness, generosity, and tenderhearted love that God bears toward the members of his family. Paul Martin agreed that confusion about grace is a mark of abusive churches and of non-Christian religions:

> Almost all former members of religious cults or extremist sects (including those that are doctrinally evangelical)

are confused about such things as the grace of God, the character of God, submission to authority, and self-denial. It is noteworthy that groups with widely varying doctrinal stances—from the Hare Krishnas to Jehovah's Witnesses—uniformly distort God's grace and character.[6]

Abusive churches practice and teach a hard, exacting, *mean* theology that is often dismissive of the place of grace in the life of the church community. To visit, join, or participate in a church that practices grace can almost make a survivor of a graceless church dizzy as she finds herself "breathing in" spiritual air with a 99 percent grace saturation, as opposed to the suffocating grace-less air of her former church. Churches that are marked by such a highly saturated grace environment are relaxed, never pushy or demanding, accepting of wherever a person might be on her spiritual path, and eager to welcome. Grace-infused churches do not exist to get something from members, but to give something good and generous and loving to all, in service to a dear Savior who gave his life for all.

To sum up, safe churches are not perfect churches. Like all churches, they comprise people who share a deep neediness for forgiveness, restoration, and community, and an even deeper appreciation for God's kindness and love. They are not full of self-satisfied, completed saints, gathered merely to keep each other company until the Lord sweeps them up to heaven. They are communities where healthy relationships are sought, where all people are respected and treated with fairness and honesty, and where the claims of Jesus Christ, as found in the Bible, are preached, taught, and offered as the means of forgiveness, acceptance, and eternal life. They are also communities whose members seek to form and maintain healthy, respectful relationships, not only between members, but also with all people. Rather than seeking the control and subjection of members, and emotionally bullying members into beliefs and behaviors that are unfamiliar, safe churches are places where everyone is granted time and space to process the claims

6. Martin, *Cult Proofing Your Kids*, 48.

and biblical practices of the Christian faith. They are places people truly *want* to wake up and go to on a Sunday morning.

Chapter 10

Some Final Thoughts
for Family and Friends . . .

SOMETIMES FAMILY AND FRIENDS of people who are embedded in abusive churches reach out to me. They report months or years of a deteriorating relationship with their family member or friend and, sadly, they are often sure the relationship is irredeemably lost. They tell of missed family events, changes in personality, plenty of theological arguing, and the constant concern for their loved one's well-being, including both physical and emotional health. If your loved one, family member, or friend is in an abusive church, here are some basic truths to remember, and some positive actions you can take so that (as far as you are concerned) the door is open for the building of a genuine (though not perfect!) relationship.

First, remember that most people leave abusive groups and cults, though they may have been in them for many years. Inevitably, the false, disingenuous personality (or self) the member developed to become a functioning, accepted member of the abusive church is finally overcome by the person's true, authentic self. As I reflect on my time in an abusive church and the process of leaving it, I see that the inmost parts of my psyche, my private thoughts and beliefs, were never really destroyed or even replaced by the outer, church-pleasing personality that I developed in my time there. No, the *real* me, the Ken that I was born as and is my core personality, was simply shut down, repressed by my attempt to fit in and avoid displeasing my leaders and fellow church members. But my authentic, true self battled for me, and eventually won.

Your friend or loved one has not really been lost; he has simply been camouflaged by the false, cultic, abusive church self that is being formed by the policies and social environment of the group. Although the control and influence of the leaders of cultic groups seems overwhelming and total, as Michael Langone has noted, it is "not absolute because ultimately most people leave cultic groups."[1] Never give up on your loved one! Never give up hope!

Second, tremendous impact for good is made in the life of the members of an abusive church when an outsider treats them with kindness, affection, and acceptance. Many of the friends, parents, and family of abusive church members attempt to argue their loved one out of the church through theological debate, attacks on the leader of the church, or the application of a good-sized serving of guilt for the loved one's abandonment of personal relationships. It is certainly understandable that a concerned parent, sibling, spouse, or friend would resort to these tactics; but the fact is, they simply do not work. By the time members of an abusive church have made the decision to join and live as fully committed members, they have long since rejected the theological rationale of outsiders and likely are convinced that their pastor's grasp of theology and logic exceeds that of outside voices. (They probably believe that *their* own grasp of those things also exceeds those voice, too!) They have come to see the abusive leader as a great man or woman of God, misunderstood by the outside, uninitiated world, as many great religious leaders of history have been.

Moreover, they have been well prepared by the abusive church leaders for the onslaught of concern, criticism, and guilt they will encounter from family and friends. (As I interact with members of abusive, cultic Christian churches, I am impressed by the organized, passionate arguments they have learned in order to defend their churches from the accusation of being cults!) However, for members to be treated with kindness, affection, and respect

---

1. Langone, *Recovery from Cults*, 9.

by their family and friends, without argument or criticism from their pastor or shaming accusations of their failure to maintain relationships, is very powerful. It makes a deep, if unacknowledged, impact on the member.

Be available to get together, anytime. Remind your loved one that she can call you, anytime, and you will always be there, no questions asked. Express affection, acceptance, and commendation for the good things she is accomplishing in her church. Perhaps she is excelling in Bible study or devoting time to service of the poor and needy. Perhaps she is becoming a person of a deeper character and integrity and is gaining social skills that did not exist before membership in the abusive church. (All of those are distinct possibilities!) Do not be shy about praising what is good. Do not withhold affection because of her abusive church. Be as present in her life as she will allow. Remind her of the love you have for her, and of the cherished memories you will always have of your relationship with her. (Deep down, she has not forgotten those memories, either!) Learn the names of her friends in the church and invite them over for dinner or a barbecue.

Do your best to rise above the tension, awkwardness, and distancing that often marks the relationships between abusive church members and their (nonmember) family and friends. Do not stop inviting her to every family event, holiday, and special occasion, even though she often does not show up. Visit her church, and avoid the temptation to be consumed with a criticism of the church, or to engage in arguing or defending your beliefs. Just visit because someone you care about belongs to that church, and you do care, after all. Walk through the doors of your loved one's church with nothing but your love, and your prayers for their good and blessing. Ask God that he would fill your soul with his Spirit of power, love, and sound thinking, and he will. Genuine love is simply more powerful than all the dogma, coercion, and religious zeal in the world and will win out in the end.

Don't be afraid to ask questions about your loved one's church, including things about it you might disagree with or be puzzled about. Just make sure you are kind, truly humble, and not intense about it. Although your loved one might not acknowledge the reasonableness and legitimacy of your questions, deep inside, your questions will rattle around and provoke her consideration. However, the questions you ask with kindness and respect have the greatest chance of remaining on her mind long after the conversation is over.

Third, family members and friends of those who are in abusive groups usually find great benefit in learning about the general processes of thought-reforming groups (such as cults and abusive churches) from an academic standpoint. It can be discomfiting to read of the horrific abuses that take place in such groups, particularly when you are imagining your loved one as a member of the same. However, it is also liberating to see that you have not been thrown into an unchartered wilderness but are simply entering a world that is new to you, and that world is widely researched and understood by professionals and survivors alike. There are numerous books and articles available that address the phenomena of spiritual abuse from a secular and Christian perspective.[2]

Fourth, survivors of abusive churches can offer much-needed affirmation and empathy. It is likely there are survivors of the abusive church to which your loved one belongs. Just having a cup of coffee with someone who *gets it* regarding abusive churches can be both powerful and empowering. Once you start asking around, somebody will know somebody who knows a person who has some knowledge of spiritual abuse, and perhaps, even of the specific group of your loved one. Do not be afraid to reach out; when you do, you'll find that you are not alone, and there is hope that your loved one will one day be restored to family and friends—and to the better angels of their nature.

2. See bibliography.

Epilogue: Why I Am Here Again

2019

THE COURTROOM OF THE Oregon Supreme Court is palatial. The walls are a rich, deeply stained wood; the windows above are ornate, stained-glass works of art. The carpeted floor contributes greatly to an expectation of quietness and seriousness. Voices project only as muffled whispers. We are waiting for the six judges who preside over Oregon's highest court to enter.

Again, there are victims in the room. My friends, family members, and attorneys are seated on one side. This time it is not warm. It is a clear, cold January day, and we are all wrapped in our winter coats. We have driven more than fifty miles for this ninety-minute event. We nod, smile, whisper *hello* as we see each other. I feel the same tightness of the chest and knotting in the stomach.

Many of the players in this saga are here again, four years after the first trial, with one notable absence: the pastor is not here. He is just a couple of miles away, but he will not be attending court today.

On the other side are the remaining members of his church, fidgeting, whispering, and waiting, as we are, for things to begin. (And yes, they are again dressed in their Sunday best.) A few are parents of their pastor's victims, here today in their two-decades-long, maniacal commitment to support their pastor instead of their own daughters.

These mothers and fathers have not spoken to their daughters—not so much as a phone call, email, birthday card, or even a *like* on Facebook—for years. One of the daughters is present, sitting next to me. Her father does not glance across the room to acknowledge her presence. As we've learned by now, that's just the way it goes with these folks. Neither blood nor marriage will supersede their commitment to their pastor.

The defense lawyer is here, at this final stop of an appeals process that he promised immediately following his client's sentencing four years ago, when a jury decided the pastor was guilty of felony sexual assault of a minor, and a judge sent him to prison for a twenty-year sentence. The defense attorney has had a long time to prepare for this day.

The assistant attorney general of the state of Oregon is here, too, ready to argue that the pastor's trial was fair, orderly, proper, and that its verdict and sentencing should be upheld.

The pastor's lawyer will argue that the trial was *not* fair or proper. Not at all. Witnesses who never should have been allowed to do so had testified against his client. All of them stated that the pastor had molested them as children. The defense lawyer argued that allowing six of the seven witnesses to testify had prejudiced the jury against his client, for six of the incidents were past the state of Oregon's statute of limitations. He will argue that the purpose of the trail was regarding the *alleged* sexual abuse of only one *alleged* victim—and every *alleged* victim should have been referred to as *alleged* victim—without exception!

As the six Supreme Court judges enter, all rise, and the next ninety minutes of carefully timed presentations, questions, and closing arguments quickly pass. There is much discussion over the failure of the Multnomah County Court to qualify all of the plaintiffs as *alleged* victims during the trial four years ago.

That is why I am here today, again . . .

~

In June, the court delivers its decision: the consistent omission of the word *alleged* to qualify the seven (alleged) victims during the initial trial may very well have prejudiced the jury against the defendant, thus depriving him of a fair trial. His case is sent back to the Multnomah County Court for retrial. At the pastor's release hearing, the county judge refuses to lower the $750,000 bail; he also requires the pastor to avoid all contact with children, and to wear a GPS monitoring device.

~

As I write on this September day, we are all awaiting the retrial, and the cruel irony of those two words, *alleged* and *victim*, are particularly haunting. They are painfully familiar to all of us who once belonged to the pastor's mad carnival of a church.

I hear the word *alleged* echo forward from thirty years ago . . . We were told then that the pastor only *allegedly* had used drugs, seduced young single women, given alcohol to teens: "Our pastor is being slandered, maligned by a jealous, disordered person. This is exactly the nature of attack that we expect the devil to make against our leaders. So remember, those are simply *allegations*, not proven facts!"

And in our little church, one was never really a *victim*—one was always *acting* like a victim. To claim to have been victimized—by anyone—was to claim incompetency and pathetic weakness:

"Don't be a victim."

"Don't buy the victim narrative."

"You're acting like a victim! *I'm* the real victim here, for having to endure your unteachable spirit, your resentment, your doubt!"

What tragic irony! Two of the (many) words that bolstered the pastor's grip of domination and abuse—which hurt so many—reappear more than twenty years later and are the words that silence the brave testimony of his victims and deliver him from justice.

Free for now, anyway, while I await a promised day when words will be weighed, judged, remembered, and perfectly employed as servants of truth, not of its enemies.

Maranatha.

End note: On January 23, 2020, a retrial subsequent to the state of Oregon appeal process, a Multnomah County, Oregon, jury found the pastor of the abusive church (to which I belonged to from 1984– 1996) guilty of the sexual abuse of a minor, and sentenced him to 160 months incarnation, without the possibility of parole.

Bibliography and further reading

Allen, A. "Impact on Children of Being Born into / Raised in a Cultic Group." *ICSA Today* 7 (2016) 17–22. http://www.icsahome.com/articles/impact-on-children-of-being-born-into-raised-in-a-cultic-group-docx.

Almendros, C., et al. "Reasons for Leaving: Psychological Abuse and Distress Reported by Former Members of Cultic Groups." *Cultic Studies Review* 8 (2019) 111–38. http://www.icsahome.com/articles/reasons-for-leaving-almendros.

Arterburn, S., and J. Felton. *Toxic Faith: Understanding and Overcoming Religious Addiction.* 1st ed. Nashville: Nelson, 1991.

Ashmun J. M. "Narcissistic Personality Disorder (NPD): DSM-IV Diagnostic Criteria." 2016. http://www.halcyon.com/jmashmun/npd/dsm-iv.html.

Bissell, H. *By Hook or By Crook: How Cults Lure Christians.* New York: McCracken, 1993.

Blimling, G. S. "The Involvement of College Students in Totalist Groups: Causes, Concerns, Legal Issues, and Policy Considerations." *Cultic Studies Journal* 7 (1990) 41–68. http://www.icsahome.com/articles/the-involvement-of-college-students-in-totalist-groups-csj-7-1.

Blue, K. *Healing Spiritual Abuse: How to Break Free from Bad Church Experiences.* 5th ed. Downers Grove: InterVarsity, 1993.

Bradshaw, R. "What Is a Cult? Definitional Preface." *ICSA Today* 6 (2015) 8–9. http://www.icsahome.com/articles/what-is-a-cult-definitional-preface.

Breese, D. *Know the Marks of a Cult: A Guide to Enable You to Quickly Detect the Basic Errors of False Religion.* Wheaton, IL: Victor, 1975.

Burks, R., et al. *Damaged Disciples: Casualties of Authoritarian Churches and the Shepherding Movement.* Grand Rapids: Zondervan, 1992.

Damgaard, N. C. "A Safe-Haven Church: An Introduction to the Basics of a Safe Religious Community." *ICSA Today* 6 (2015) 2–7. http://www.icsahome.com/articles/a-safe-haven-church-an-introduction-to-the-basics-of-a-safe-religious-community.

De Canonville, C. L. *The Three Faces of Evil.* 1st ed. Stouffville, ON: Black Card, 2015.

Diagnostic and Statistical Manual of Mental Disorders: DSM-5. 5th ed. Washington, DC: American Psychiatric Publishing, 2013.

Dowhower, R. L. "Religion versus Cult." Excerpted from R. L. Dowhower, "Guidelines for Clergy," in *Recovery from Cults,* edited by Michael D. Langone, 251–62. New York: Norton, 1993. http://www.icsahome.com/articles/religion-versus-cult-dowhower.

———. "The Results of the International Cultic Studies Association's 2008 Questionnaire." *ICSA Today* 4 (2013) 10–11. Available at https://drive.google.com/file/d/oB4dmoPK1tYNjbllMdjRfMG1OR3c/edit.

Duncan, W. *I Can't Hear God Anymore: Life in a Dallas Cult.* Garland, TX: VM Life Resources, 2015.

Enroth, R. M. *Churches That Abuse.* Grand Rapids: Zondervan, 1992.

———. "Dysfunctional Churches." *Cult Observer* 9 (1992). https://www.icsahome.com/articles/dysfunctional-churches-enroth.

———. *Recovering from Churches That Abuse.* Grand Rapids: Zondervan, 1994.

Friberg, T., et al. *Analytical Lexicon to the Greek New Testament.* Baker's Greek New Testament Library. Grand Rapids: Baker, 2000.

Giambalvo, C. "International Churches of Christ: Introduction." Originally presented at an International Cultic Studies Association Recovery Workshop. http://www.icsahome.com/articles/international-churches-of-christ-introduction.

———. "An Open Letter to Clergy regarding Helping Former Members of Abusive Churches or Cults." *ICSA Today* 3 (2012) 6–8. http://www.icsahome.com/articles/letterclergy.

Goldberg, L. "Reflections on Marriage and Children after the Cult." *Cultic Studies Review* 2 (2003) 9–29. http://www.icsahome.com/articles/reflections-on-marriage-and-children-after-the-cult.

Green, M. E. "Post-Cult Financial Recovery." *ICSA Today* 1 (2010) 24–27. http://www.icsahome.com/articles/post-cult-financial-recovery-greene.

Hassan, S. *Combating Cult Mind Control: The #1 Best-Selling Guide to Protection, Rescue, and Recovery from Destructive Cults.* Newton, MA: Freedom of Mind, 2015.

———. *Releasing the Bonds: Empowering People to Think for Themselves.* 1st ed. Somerville, MA: Aitan, 2000.

Hutchinson, J. *Out of the Cults and into the Church.* Everett, WA: Cross and Pen, 2012.

Jacobs, J. "Deconversion from Religious Movements: An Analysis of Charismatic Bonding and Spiritual Commitment." *Journal for the Scientific Study of Religion* 26 (1987) 294–308.

Jefferson, C. *The Minister as Shepherd: The Privileges and Responsibilities of Pastoral Leadership.* Fort Washington, PA: Christian Literature Crusade, 2006.

Johnson, D., and J. VanVonderen. *The Subtle Power of Spiritual Abuse: Recognizing and Escaping Spiritual Manipulation and False Spiritual Authority within the Church.* Reprint. Minneapolis: Bethany House, 2005.

Kelly, K. *The Making of a Disciple in the International Churches of Christ.* International Cultic Studies Association, n.d. http://www.icsahome. com/articles/the-making-of-a-disciple-in-the-international-churches-of-christ.

Langone, M. D. "Advice for Church Authorities." International Cultic Studies Association, n.d. https://www.icsahome.com/elibrary/topics/catholic/advice.

———. "Are 'Sound' Theology and Cultism Mutually Exclusive?" *Cult Observer* 11 (1994) 21–22. https://www.icsahome.com/articles/are--sound--theology-and-cultism-mutually-exclusive-langone-co-11-9-10.

———. "Characteristics Associated with Cultic Groups—Revised." *ICSA Today* 6 (2015) 10. http://www.icsahome.com/articles/characteristics.

———. "Clergy." International Cultic Studies Association, n.d. http://www. icsahome.com/elibrary/studyguides/clergy.

———, ed. "Cults, Evangelicals, and the Ethics of Social Influence." Special issue of *Cultic Studies Journal* 2 (1985). Available at https://drive.google. com/file/d/0B4dmoPK1tYNjS3R2cG5ZVmt1Zmc/edit.

———. "Deception, Dependency, and Dread." International Cultic Studies Association, n.d. https://www.icsahome.com/articles/deception--dependency--and-dread-langone.

———. "The Definitional Ambiguity of Cult." *ICSA Today* 6 (2015) 6–7. http:// www.icsahome.com/articles/definitionalambiguity.

———. *Recovery from Cults: Help for Victims of Psychological and Spiritual Abuse.* New York: Norton, 1995.

———. "Research Survey on Spiritual Abuse." Spiritual Abuse Resources, a program of the International Cultic Studies Association, 2016. https:// www.spiritualabuseresources.com/articles/research-survey-on-spiritual-abuse.

Lifton, R. J. "Cult Formation." *Cultic Studies Journal* 8 (1991) 1–6. Reprinted with permission from the February 1991 issue of the *Harvard Mental Health Letter* (abstract added). http://www.icsahome.com/articles/cult-formation-lifton-csj-8-1-1991.

———. *Thought Reform and the Psychology of Totalism: A Study of "Brainwashing" in China.* Chapel Hill: University of North Carolina Press, 2012.

Martin, P. R. *Cult Proofing Your Kids.* Grand Rapids: Zondervan, 1993.

Martin, S. *The Heresy of Mind Control: Recognizing Con Artists, Tyrants, and Spiritual Abusers in Leadership.* Nashville: ACW, 2009.

Martin, W. *The Kingdom of the Cults.* Grand Rapids: Zondervan, 1955.

McIntosh, G. L., and S. D. Rima. *Overcoming the Dark Side of Leadership: How to Become an Effective Leader by Confronting Potential Failures.* Rev. ed. Grand Rapids: Baker, 2007.

Pile, L. A. "Choosing a Church after a Painful Experience." International Cultic Studies Association, n.d. http://www.icsahome.com/articles/choosing-a-church-pile.

Rabbinowitz, N. S. "Matthew 23:2–4: Does Jesus Recognize the Authority of the Pharisees and Does He Endorse Their Halakhah?" *Journal of the Evangelical Theological Society* 46 (2003) 423–30.

Richardson, R. W. *Creating a Healthier Church: Family Systems Theory, Leadership and Congregational Life.* Minneapolis: Fortress, 1996.

Shaw, D. *Traumatic Narcissism: Relational Systems of Subjugation.* 1st ed. Mahwah, NJ: Routledge, 2013.

Singer, M. T. "Coming Out of the Cults." International Cultic Studies Association. Excerpted from "Coming Out of the Cults," *Psychology Today,* January 1979. http://www.icsahome.com/articles/coming-out-of-cults-singer.

Singer, M. T., and Lifton, R. J. *Cults in Our Midst: The Continuing Fight against Their Hidden Menace.* 1st ed. San Francisco: Jossey-Bass, 2003.

Sire, J. W. *Scripture Twisting: 20 Ways the Cults Misread the Bible.* Downers Grove: InterVarsity, 1980.

Smedes, L. B. *Shame and Grace: Healing the Shame We Don't Deserve.* Lexington, KY: HarperOne, 2009.

Stein, A. *Terror, Love & Brainwashing: Attachment in Cults and Totalitarian Systems.* New York: Routledge, 2017.

Tchividjian, B. "7 Ways to Welcome Abuse Survivors in Our Churches." Godly Response to Abuse in the Christian Environment. Originally published May 16, 2014, Religion News Service. https://www.netgrace.org/resources/7-ways-to-welcome-survivors?rq=7%20Ways%20to%20Welcome%20Abuse%20Survivors%20in%20Our%20Churches.

Tobias, M. L., and J. Lalich. *Captive Hearts, Captive Minds: Freedom and Recovery from Cults and Abusive Relationships.* Alameda, CA: Hunter House, 1994.

Tozer, A. W. *The Pursuit of God: The Human Thirst for the Divine.* Hannibal, MO: WingSpread, 2007.

US Department of Veterans Affairs. "Complex PTSD." https://www.ptsd.va.gov/professional/treat/essentials/complex_ptsd.asp.

Vaknin, S. *Malignant Self-Love: Narcissism Revisited.* Edited by L. Rangelovska. Rev. ed. Skopje, Republic of Macedonia: Narcissus, 2015.

Yeakley, F. R., Jr., ed. *Discipling Dilemma: A Study of the Discipling Movement among Churches of Christ.* 1st ed. Nashville: Gospel Advocate, 1988.

Zimbardo, P. G. "What Messages Are behind Today's Cults?" *American Psychological Association Monitor* 28 (1997) 14–65.

Made in the USA
Monee, IL
25 March 2021